THE
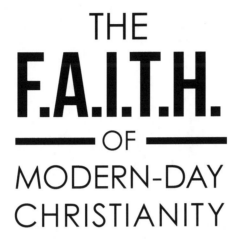
F.A.I.T.H.
— OF —
MODERN-DAY
CHRISTIANITY

DR. DALE I. MORGAN

BALBOA.
PRESS
A DIVISION OF HAY HOUSE

Balboa Press books may be ordered through booksellers or by contacting:

Balboa Press
A Division of Hay House
1663 Liberty Drive
Bloomington, IN 47403
www.balboapress.com
1 (877) 407-4847

Print information available on the last page.

ISBN: 978-1-5043-7259-6 (sc)
ISBN: 978-1-5043-7260-2 (hc)
ISBN: 978-1-5043-7258-9 (e)

Library of Congress Control Number: 2016921313

Balboa Press rev. date: 12/22/2016

This book is dedicated to my wife, Yuni, who encouraged me all throughout the writing. Even when I had had several surgeries during the time I labored on it, she never gave up on me and encouraged me to keep going.

Also to all my church people at Dorcas Baptist Church, you all know who you are, for having the confidence and trust in me to shepherd you for the past 10 years. God bless all of you!

To my friends, acquaintances and all my brothers and sisters in Christ, thank you for all your prayers while I was laboring on this book. I certainly could not have done it without them.

Most importantly, I want to thank God for the guidance he has given me over the period of time that it took to write this book. To Him goes all the glory! Amen!

Contents

Introduction...ix

Chapter 1   Fear 1

Chapter 2   Apathy...23

Chapter 3   Ignorance...45

Chapter 4   Tolerance 73

Chapter 5   Hypocrisy..85

Introduction

All passages of scripture quoted in this book come directly from the King James Version of the bible.

By no means whatsoever is this book written to condemn or demean Christianity. On the contrary, I have given my life to Christ since becoming a Christian in October of 1993. It just so happens that I was saved in a church that believed in the "old fashioned" type of preaching and teaching. I was not around during the revivals of D.L. Moody, R.A. Torrey and Billy Sunday. But the one thing I have noticed is that we have had a lack of preachers like this in our modern day and time. I have given many years of thought as to why there is no revival in our churches today and I have come to the conclusion that we are just not doing Christianity in the way it was meant to be done. We've become machines instead of loving, caring Christians with the attitude of, "Well, I just don't want to get involved with it." It seems as if Christianity isn't the "In" thing to do anymore. This book is meant to try and stir some enthusiasm, and perhaps, if necessary, some anger, into the hearts of Christians all over the world. I believe that there are two factors involved.

First and foremost, I blame the people in the pulpit for watering down the Word of God. Not all preachers want to preach about the blood, the sacrifices and what it really takes to be a Christian in these times. Either they are afraid of offending someone in the congregation, or, as we'll discuss in the final chapter of this book, they don't believe one word of what they are preaching. It's a sad situation for sure. They feel uneasy when they get out of their comfort zone. It seems as if they feel threatened.

Although I don't know of any pastor who has not gotten discouraged a time or two in his ministry, myself included, if a preacher/pastor has a fear of insulting someone or hurting someone's feelings because of what the Bible says, it's time to step back and take a look and see if you are really doing what God has called you to do. This not only applies to pastors, but to all Christians. Soul winning is a must in any church. I have a young couple in my church, age 19 and 18 that go out every Friday night to the local college campus and hand out tracts. What a great ministry that is becoming. We even got a young man from Nepal into our church to hear the preaching of God's Word because of these two fine young folks.

The second reason we don't have revival is because of pure laziness. This is another attribute of both pastors and lay people alike. The pastor doesn't study and so his sermons are shoddy, haphazard and boring. Vance Havner once said "Some churches start at eleven o'clock sharp and end at twelve o'clock dull." It's difficult to keep a congregation's attention span for more than 30 minutes, and one will not even keep it that long if the sermon is dry and empty. Church members also are guilty of the same fault. They don't want to study their Bible, and consequently, whatever the pastor says makes no sense to them and they quite frankly, are bored to tears.

I see Christianity in dire straits at the present time. Liberalism, Pluralism, Secular Humanism, and New Ageism have all replaced "fire and brimstone" preaching in our pulpits today. Consequently, the preachers who do preach that the Devil is real and hell is hot are looked upon as "bible thumping fanatics." Don't misunderstand what I'm saying here. I still believe that there are still many preachers and churches who unashamedly, confidently and proudly preach the Gospel of Jesus Christ. But more often than not, these are the exception and not the rule.

I have broken down the five main reasons Christianity is in a lull right now. Notice I don't say "failing!" Christianity will never fail. Christians fail, but the war has already been won. We may have lost a few battles, but for all intents and purposes, the war is over. It's just that a lot of Christians have stopped fighting. The five main reasons why Christianity is taking a back seat to other cult religions and political views are as follows, thus The F.A.I.T.H. of Modern Day Christianity:

Fear – What do Christians fear most and why?

Apathy – Some Christians are lazy and some just don't care.

Ignorance – Most of this ignorance of Christianity is "self-inflicted."

Tolerance – Putting up with sin just because it's the fashionable thing to do.

Hypocrisy – When your walk doesn't match your talk.

We will see what the reactions are from readers and what steps will be taken to remedy the situation to build them up spiritually, or will it be just another book on the shelf? I fully expect to raise the ire in some Christian's hearts with this book. Some may call me a religious fanatic, some may call me a religious zealot and may I say feel free to call me whatever you wish? I call myself a Christian who loves Jesus Christ and who wants the entire world to know that He loves them too, and died for them on the cross of Calvary.

As we move in to chapter one, please try to see that I am writing this out of love for Christians all over the world, as brothers and sisters in Christ. I have dear friends serving the Lord in Ogbomosho, Nigeria, Melukavumattom, India and in China. I have a heart for missions, but missions begin at home. Having said that, the Church of Jesus Christ is my mission field right now and I'm trying desperately to open the eyes of sleeping Christians and raise an awareness in them. If we don't take steps to "patch the holes" in our Gospel ship, we will slowly sink into the depths of nowhere.

It my comments tend to ruffle a few feathers, so be it! I'm speaking what's on my heart. If you see yourself within the pages of this book, take it seriously but not personally. It is meant to enlighten and not condemn. A doctor who discovers that his patient has a serious illness and does not tell the patient is not much of a doctor. Sometimes the truth may hurt a little bit, but, as far as spiritual matters go, truth is always right.

Chapter One

FEAR

Merriam-Webster's Dictionary defines fear as "to be afraid of (something or someone); to expect or worry about (something bad or unpleasant); to be afraid and worried.[1] We all have certain fears or phobias that plague us at one time or another. However, when it comes to the things of God, this should never be the case. 2 Timothy 1:7 tells us, *"For God hath not given us the spirit of fear; but of power, and of love, and of a sound mind."* When it comes to the church, God's people have a mindset that says, "If you're afraid to say it, wait for someone else to say it." Or, "If you're afraid to do it, wait for someone else to do it."

Fear of Ostracism

One of the biggest fears of Christians today is other Christians. When a Christian dares to break from the "norm", (by that I mean from the Apostasy of Christendom today), he or she is going to be ostracized. Not only Christians, but the Church in general will come down hard on anyone who varies from the "don't rock the boat" mentality in churches today. How dare anyone criticize the church or

---

[1]   Merriam-Webster Online Dictionary 2016

the pastor or anyone else in the name of Christ? Some churches are so far removed from the true Gospel that there is little or no hope of it coming back on the right track. But the main problem is that no one will speak out.

I have been in the position of the proverbial "Red-headed stepchild" in my "denomination" (I totally loathe the use of that word) on several occasions. If I would call them on something which I thought was wrong, I would either get no answer or be labeled as a "trouble maker." Ostracism doesn't bother me, but there are others who, in their extreme need to be a part of the church, no matter what the doctrine or policy, would never say or do anything which would insult or demean the church or its leadership. I'm not talking about just being a troublemaker here. On the contrary, I believe it's every Christian's duty to ask questions about something he or she doesn't believe is right or doctrinal, or maybe they just don't understand. On the other hand, they won't move and go somewhere else either. This church or that church has become their pacifier and they are not going to let go of it, no matter how much harm it does to their spiritual life.

There is in each of us a deep seated need to belong, and this is good as far as it goes. Indeed, the Bible itself tells us in Hebrews 10:25, *"Not forsaking the assembling of ourselves together, as the manner of some is; but exhorting one another: and so much the more, as ye see the day approaching."* We have the *"assembling"* part down fairly well; but we are sorely lacking in the *"exhorting"* department. It is such a tragedy today that, when we know that something isn't right, we turn our backs and act like everything is alright for fear of the repercussions that speaking out might bring.

I am not talking about petty things here. I do believe that complaining is an art that some people have mastered very well. Indeed, I have seen people leave a church because they don't like the color of the new carpet that was installed; or so and so got to sing a solo instead of them. If people get their feelings hurt, they need to "man-up" and take the biblical rebuke like an adult. Too many people leave churches simply because they got their feelings hurt. But what

I'm talking about here is speaking out on things that prevent the church from carrying out the Great Commission that Christ gave us before He left. If done in a loving way, constructive criticism is a valuable tool in churches today. Proverbs 27:6 states, *"Faithful are the wounds of a friend."*

Fear of Change

My first pastorate was a very small country church founded in 1879. They were the most wonderful people any pastor could have hoped to have ever had. They were not growing and the lay leaders (i.e. deacons) stepped on every suggestion that I made to get the church to grow. They were content and resisted change because it would mean that their church wouldn't be the same as it was for the past 50 years or so. It is evident that we expect every Sunday to be the same. The same people in the same pew, the same type of message preached every Sunday and the same warm fuzzy feeling as we are going home. I stayed there almost 5 years and did everything I could to make them grow, but to no avail. It was an attitude of, "This is the way it has been since I've been here and I like it this way." New people mean new ideas and new ideas are frightening to some people. It is a dangerous thing to become comfortable with one's Christianity. Once content, we tend not to move forward.

I do believe that sometimes, too much change is not good also. I've seen new pastors come into a church and, without even assessing the situation, jump in with both feet changing this program and that program, and before long, the entire system is out of balance. But the fact still remains that if a church is not growing, not winning souls to Christ, not changing lives and not convicting hearts, something is dreadfully wrong. There is a problem in a church that is not doing all of the things I just listed, yet, no one will take the initiative to fix the problem; not even the pastor. Pastors tend to be fearful of change also. Not all preachers want to preach about the blood, sacrifice and what it really takes to be a Christian in these perilous times. I had a small Chihuahua and when he was tired, he looked for the most comfortable place he could find, and when he found it, he planted himself there until he was good and ready to get up. This is what pastors are doing today. They find a comfortable situation and "plant" themselves there because it feels good to them. They don't want to risk ruffling feathers and as a result, they tell the people what they WANT to hear as opposed to what they NEED to hear. They feel uneasy when they get out of their comfort zone. It seems as if they feel threatened.

I don't know of any pastor who has not gotten discouraged a time or two in his ministry, myself included; but if one is at the point of being afraid of insulting or hurting someone's feelings simply because he is preaching the gospel, it's time to step back and take a look and see if you are really doing what God has called you to do. This not only applies to pastors, but to all Christians. Soul winning is not a spiritual gift. On the contrary, it is a direct command of Jesus Christ. He said in Matthew 28:19, "*Go YE*" (emphasis mine). That was directed to all of us who claim the name of Christ.

Fear of Responsibility

Some people thrive on responsibility while others avoid it like the plague. I've heard it said that 90% of all the work in a church is done by 10% of the members. This is probably an accurate estimation. Why most Christians shun responsibility is a puzzling question, but there are answers.

One reason is that most people have a feeling of inadequacy. Little do they know that any pastor, deacon or lay worker who doesn't feel inadequate to carry out the work of Christ does not really understand the importance of his or her work. Nobody is perfect and feeling inadequate should be expected. But through prayer, fasting and supplication, those feelings will go away. One of the first things I learned in seminary was just how much I didn't know. It was a very humbling experience and I have never forgotten it.

Another reason people fear responsibility is that they are afraid that it will put too much work on them which will interfere with their personal lives. It seems as if these people want all the benefits of Christianity (i.e. salvation, heaven, blessings, etc) but don't really want to have to do anything to get them. It's like they are saying, "Ok, God! I'll take your salvation, I want your blessings and your love, but don't tell me how to live my life; don't' tell me how to raise my children, and don't tell me how to spend my money. I'll take care of all of that. Oh, and by the way, don't expect me to do anything for you, either. You just go over in your little corner, and if I need you, I'll ring your bell." People like this shun teaching Sunday School because there is too much time involved in studying God's Word, and they don't want to be "bogged down" every Sunday because it will interfere with their plans. These are the people who prefer the golf course, the lake or the mountains or even sleeping in on Sunday instead of the sanctuary. These are the ones whom you may see on Sunday morning, but rarely on Sunday night and never on Wednesday night. These are also the ones who will criticize the ones who do most of the work and call them "power hungry." They tend to see anyone who does a lot of work around the church as a threat, yet won't raise one finger to help in any way. I pray for them because they are cheating themselves out of the joy that comes with serving the Lord.

Let me just invoke a word here about the "power hungry" people. It is apparent that there are people in churches that do, in fact, want to have more of a say in the business and operation of the church than any of the other people, and they inflict more harm to the church than any of the others I have listed above. I have pastor friends who have told me horror stories about "family run" churches. There is this family or that family that has more relatives in the church than anyone else and they will control every aspect of the church business. If they don't get their way, they will make life totally miserable for the pastor and force him to resign, or they will stop tithing and send the church into financial ruin. This causes more in-fighting in the church than any other problem and makes it almost impossible for the church to carry out the Great Commission, let alone, get new members to join the church. People and families like this need to pray and get their spiritual lives back where they need to be with God and stop thinking about themselves and stop thinking that the church cannot operate without their pushing and shoving. This is normally the case in the smaller churches, but it happens in the largest of churches also. What I would suggest to anyone reading this book is to highlight this section with a bright yellow highlighter pen and give it to the offending families. Then they can see how really selfish everyone else thinks they are. However, the best way is the biblical way, which is to confront them openly and tell them. If that fails, go with two or three members and confront them again. Lastly, if all else fails, take it before the church.

Fear of Non-Denominationalism

Although I was saved in an independent Baptist church, the first two churches that I pastored were Southern Baptist Churches. It seemed like the more I stayed in the Southern Baptist Convention, the more discouraged I became with them. When you try to get people to break away from the structure of the hierarchy, you always meet with resistance. Once again, it is the need to belong that keeps people from moving out on their own and taking control of their spirituality instead of it being dictated to you from someone else. The Southern Baptists, the United Methodists, the Presbyterian Church USA, the Episcopal Church, and the Roman Catholic Church all have these hierarchies that dictate to them in matters pursuant to their respective beliefs. It seems as if no one except the hierarchies is capable of making decisions concerning the local churches. All of these will be discussed in chapter four.

Yet, for a church to be biblical, it has to make its own decisions, appoint its own staff and dictate its own rules. Jesus Christ told us to go and make disciples of all nations, but he didn't say, "Establish a coalition of churches so you can keep your thumbs on them." True, Paul visited many churches and told them of the error of their ways, but he never tried to appoint a larger organization over them. It is also true that the disciples and Paul met at Jerusalem to discuss whether or not to require the saved gentiles to be circumcised (Acts 15), but they never invoked all the "man made" rules that you have in the present day Councils, Conventions and Presbyteries in these present day churches. Each church had its own leadership and operated independent of all others.

You can't, however, convince most church members that the best way to go is to become an independent church. It's the old adage, "My daddy was a Southern Baptist or a Methodist, or what ever, and I'm not going to change." These churches pour dollars upon dollars into the upper echelons for them to do, in reality, what God has told the local church to do. It's a means of escape for the churches. If they give their money to the larger organization, they feel that it exempts them from having to do anything else. If you ask the average Southern Baptist if his or her church supports missions, the answer that you would get most of the time is, "Oh yes, we give to the Cooperative Program." In reality, only about twenty percent of all Cooperative Program giving goes to missions. Even if a church does give to a larger organization, they should still have their own missions program, and support individual missionaries.

Some may say that I am advocating a total rebellion against the large church organizations. Although I believe the word "rebellion" is a bit strong, churches should, in fact, take a closer look at the large entities and make sure that it is in the best interest for their particular church to stay. Chances are that it is not in their best interest. The reasons for this are that when an organization becomes too large, the smaller churches get left out of most of the programs and decision making. Also, when a staff so large is needed that more of the money is used to pay salaries than for building God's kingdom, it's time to sit back and reflect on just where the money is going. Large staffs also make it more vulnerable to those who want to change the beliefs or doctrines of the organization to get in and start promoting a totally different agenda.

Despite all of this, most people won't release their hold on the title of Denominationalism. They have this fear that they cannot operate independently. They just overlook all the shortcomings with the hope that things will get better and good things are just around the corner. They are only fooling themselves because things never get better until someone realizes that things are getting worse, and then take action to resolve the problem.

Fear of Saying "No"

In the world we live in today, as our parents wanted only the best for us, we, in turn, want only the best for our children. The problem with this logic is that we live in a much more technological world today then when I was a child. I grew up in the early fifties and sixties, when twenty-five cents was the standard allowance for a 10 year old, if your parents could afford it. Times have certainly changed. It seems as though children as young as 7 years old have their own cell phones and their own computers. Technology is great, right? Not necessarily! I believe the main reason that a 7 year old child has a cell phone is because "all" his or her friends have one and we can't let the other kids have something our child doesn't have. What this does is teach our children at a very early age that it is important to "Keep up with the Jones' at all costs and don't let anyone get an edge on you in this competitive world in which we live."

We are raising a generation of spoiled brats in the United States and somewhere, somehow, it has to stop. Just because "everyone else has one" is not an excuse to go and buy your children their hearts desire. I have known families who are on welfare and food stamps and yet all of their children had cell phones, computers and iPads. That is totally absurd. When a child is old enough to pay for a cell phone, and there is nothing the child needs that is more important than owning a cell phone, then let him/her get one. The problem is that parents let the children compete with one another not thinking about the repercussions of the situation; and the repercussions are mind boggling. It is to the point now that children spend more time on their cell phones with all the "Apps" and social media that they rush through homework assignments and take little or no time to do proper studying. It seems as if we are raising a generation of technological morons who know all about video games, what a cell phone can and can't do, what the latest trend on social media is, but can't find China on a world map. Is it any wonder that in a recent survey, children in the United States placed an embarrassing 25th out of 40 nations in mathematics and science for 15 year old students?

Not only that, but we are raising the most sissified generation of spoiled brats this nation has ever seen. It's a total embarrassment to see college age "children" crying and running to a "safe space" on campus simply because someone said something that hurt their feelings or that they considered offensive. My goodness parents, if your child went to college that way, shame on you! If the college turned them that way, shame on them.

What am I saying here? What I'm saying is that parents need to take a more active role in their children's lives. Not just their education; in all aspects of their lives. Parents have a huge responsibility to raise their children ***in the nurture and admonition of the Lord*** as we are commanded to do in Ephesians 6:4. The word "***nurture***" there means *discipline* and the word "***admonition***" means *training*. Hilary Clinton stated at the Democratic National Convention in 1996, "And we have learned that to raise a happy, healthy and hopeful child, it takes a family, it takes teachers, it takes clergy, it takes business people, it takes community leaders, it takes those who protect our health and safety, it takes all of us. Yes, it takes a village." Contrary to what the liberal politicians may tell you, it's not the school's job to raise your children. It's not the church's job to raise your children. It's not the day care center's job to raise your children. It's not even grandma and grandpa's job to raise your children. It's your job as parents to raise your own children. We are shirking our responsibilities as parents thinking that we can turn our children loose in the wilderness of this world and expect them to survive. Many parents have done just that and then they wonder why their child started on drugs, or why the child got pregnant or why they drink alcohol.

Too many parents let their children come and go as they please, go with anyone they please, stay out as late as they please and give them anything they want. Not only that, but they let their children talk to them like they were the servants and the children are the masters of the household. There is a total lack of discipline and respect in the home in this day and age and it carries over into the educational and social realm. Children are told in school that if their parents hit them, they are to tell someone and the parents most likely will have to spend thousands of dollars on legal fees defending their right to punish their child. Some people do, in fact, go beyond the reasonable limit when it comes to punishing their children, but these are the exceptions, and not normally the rule. The bible tells us in Proverbs 13:24, *"**He that spareth his rod hateth his son: but he that loveth him chasteneth him betimes**."* We have people who have never had children trying to tell us how to raise our children. A spanking never does irreparable harm to a child. On the contrary, it develops the child's respect for authority. Teachers have to cope with children who act up in class and absolutely dare the teacher to do anything about it. When the child is disciplined in school, the parents will do anything they can to defend their "precious baby" because he or she can do no wrong. It's always some other students fault; it's the rules in the school's fault or it's the teacher's fault. But it's never the child's fault. It's to the point now that we are raising a generation of children where both boys and girls are whiney little brats. It's even come the point where college students, (yes, I said college students) need a "safe space" to run to if they feel threatened about things such as a chalk writing on the sidewalk. I have never seen such a sissified panty waisted generation as we have now in our schools. We're not raising men and women anymore, we're raising robotic "stand-ins" for the human race.

As a person who has taught school, I can tell you that you can surely tell the difference between children who were brought up in a Christian family and went to church on a regular basis as opposed to those who weren't. Now I realize that not all Christian children are perfect, and not all non-Christian children are bad; but the facts are there to see.

Parents, you need to take an active role in your child's life. Be there for your children. Too many parents today are trying to be friends with their children instead of being parents. Your children have plenty of friends. Be a parent! Stop trying to pass the buck of responsibility to someone else and raise your children according to what God's Word says. Children are on loan to us from God and we have an obligation to be responsible parents, raising them in the *"nurture and admonition of the Lord."*

Fear of Speaking Out on Issues of Importance

This is an important issue that needs to be addressed here and in the chapter on Tolerance. Social issues need to be addressed, if not in the media, then in the church. Pastors need to keep on top of social issues that have a direct effect on the church family.

Abortion

Abortion seems to only come up in January of every year on "National Right to Life Sunday." I am happy that we do set aside one Sunday every year to bring attention to the problem; however, abortions don't just happen once a year; they happen every day.

The Supreme Court of the United States of America has taken it upon itself to legislate morality. According to Lifenews.com, since Roe v. Wade in 1973, nearly 60,000,000 abortions have been performed. That averages out to 3,849 abortions per day. In 2007, of the 1,206,200 abortions performed in the United States, 60,310 were performed on girls 15 years of age and younger. Our public schools are handing out condoms but refuse to teach abstinence.

Although I do not believe it is the church's responsibility to teach sex education, I do believe that the church does have a responsibility to ensure that parents fully understand that they (parents) are responsible for educating their children in this important matter. Any parent who would allow a government run school system to "indoctrinate" their children in such an important area of their lives need not complain when one of their children becomes sexually active at 10 or 11 years of age. Sex education should begin and end with the parents; not the public schools or even the church.

Parents need to take the time and explain these things to their children in the Biblical sense. Public schools will never teach abstinence, so it is up to the parents to teach it.

I will also state here that anyone who votes for a candidate who supports abortion is just as guilty of killing an unborn child as the candidate who voted for abortion and the doctor who performed the abortion. I get so sick of women who say, "What I do to my body is my business." That's very true, but what you do to the body of the unborn child inside of you is murder. Pastors, who will speak for that innocent child if we don't?

Homosexuality

Let me say before I get started on this that Jesus has commanded that we love these people. Indeed, I do love them, but I am not commanded to love their lifestyle, or accept their way of living their lives. Nor am I commanded to remain silent on it. We will also talk more about this agenda in the chapter on Tolerance. But for right now, pastors also need to speak out against the Gay and Lesbian agenda which is being forced down the throats of Americans. In July of 2011, California Governor Jerry Brown signed into law SB 48 – FAIR Education Act. This bill would add lesbian, gay, bisexual, and transgender (LGBT) to the existing list of underrepresented cultural and ethnic groups that are required to be included in textbooks and other instructional materials in schools. This would ensure that LGBT Americans are recognized for their important historical contributions to the economic, political, and social development of California. This means that they are to teach about contributions which gay and lesbians made to our society. It is not about contributions that "people" make. It just matters if they are gay or lesbian. To be fair, why not have "Heterosexual History"? All the contributions made by heterosexuals should be taught also. If they are looking for equal rights, it would only seem fair to give equal time to both sides. The bill was introduced in the California Legislature by a gay activist. The reason I brought this up is that most parents are not aware that things like this are going on in the public-school systems. Today it is in California. Where will it be tomorrow? Maybe in Iowa, Illinois, New York? If people do not keep up with the goings on in the educational systems in their states, it will surely come.

Islam

One of the most important issues threatening our country and Christianity today is Islam. Once again, I reiterate, Jesus has commanded all of us to love these people also. I do! However, once again I don't have to like or accept their lifestyle in any way, shape or form, nor do I have to remain silent about it. According to the New World Encyclopedia, Muhammad was born 570 AD in Mecca and died June 8, 632 in Medina. Both Mecca and Medina are cities in the Hejaz region of present day Saudi Arabia. He was a merchant in Mecca when, in 610 AD at about the age of 40, while meditating in a cave, Muhammad says he experienced a vision from the angel Gabriel, who commanded him to memorize and recite the verses subsequently collected as the Qur'an. Muhammad said that the Angel Gabriel told him he would be the last of the prophets to mankind. Jesus had predicted these things when He stated in Matthew 24:5 *"For many shall come in my name, saying, I am Christ; and shall deceive many."* Some say that Islam is a religion of peace. Some say Islam is a religion of violence. I share the latter view because I myself have read the Koran (or the Qur'an). The Council on American Islamic Relations (CAIR) will tell you that we "misinterpret" the Koran on this issue. If that is the case, millions of Muslims also "misinterpret" the Koran. Pastors will not address the issue because our government, in its "infinite" wisdom, has declared that to call Islam a religion of violence is nothing less than "hate speech." Let me just quote from the Koran. "Take not the Jews and Christians for friends ... slay the idolaters [infidels] wherever ye find them....Fight against those who ... believe not in Allah nor the Last Day" (Sura 5:51; 9:5, 29, 41). "Believers! wage war against such of the infidels as are your neighbours, and let them find you rigorous: and know that God is with those who fear him." (Sura 9:123): To Islam, an "infidel" is someone other than of the Islamic faith. They preach this in their mosques and no one says anything about it. However, if a pastor says that Islam is a violent religion, they are being vilified as "hate mongers." I know that Jesus said in Matthew 5:43-44: *43 Ye have heard that it hath been said, Thou shalt love thy neighbour, and hate thine enemy. 44 But I say unto you, Love your enemies, bless them that curse you, do good to them that hate you, and pray for them which despitefully use you, and persecute you.* I do indeed love the Muslim people, but I do not love their religion, their doctrine and their ideology of wanting to destroy all who disagree with them.

I also believe that it's every Christian's right to be able to protect themselves and their families against any form of aggression. If Jesus didn't agree with that, why would he tell his disciples in Luke 22:36, *Then said he unto them, But now, he that hath a purse, let him take it, and likewise his scrip: and he that hath no sword, let him sell his garment, and buy one.*

But He also said in Luke 11:21-22: *When a strong man armed keepeth his palace, his goods are in peace: But when a stronger than he shall come upon him, and overcome him, he taketh from him all his armour wherein he trusted, and divideth his spoils.* Jesus was talking about Satan in this passage but the ramifications are still the same. A safe home comes as a result of being stronger than one who would break in to that home.

With the recent acts of violence against a Roman Catholic Priest who was beheaded in his church in Normandy, France, the shootings in Orlando, Florida and San Bernardino, California, our president has refused to call the perpetrators exactly what they are; Radical Islam. The mainstream media, CBS, ABC, NBC, CNN, and even Fox News will not report all the heinous atrocities perpetrated by the radical Islamic extremists, and our own president and the administration panders to them at every opportunity. Hopefully the new administration will take a firmer stand against this on rush of immigration from these very countries who want nothing more than world domination.

New York TV executive Muzzammil "Mo" Hassan, constantly beat and abused his wife, Aasiya, and finally, after she filed for divorce, promptly beheaded her in February 2009, in what they called an "honor killing." It was a heinous crime to be sure, but instead of getting the death penalty, what punishment did Hassan receive? 25 years to life in prison for second degree murder. In April 2011, Faleh Hassan Almaleki was also found guilty of second degree murder in the October 2009 death of his 20 year-old daughter Noor Almaleki, by running over her in a Jeep. This was also described as an "honor killing" because he felt his daughter was becoming "too westernized." His sentence; 34½ years in prison. Why were these both declared 2nd degree murder? By definition, first degree murder is planned, preparations were done to initiate the act and in the end it was successfully carried out. The act was done to literally end one's life. On the contrary, second degree murder is defined in most jurisdictions as an unplanned type of murder. These are acts that were done and were likely to cause an end to one's life. In the simplest terms, any murder that does not fall under first degree is automatically under the lower degrees usually in the second degree murder category. It takes planning to wait for your wife to show up at work and then behead her. It takes planning to go where you know your daughter is and run over her with a Jeep. The justice system is pandering to the Muslims so as not to offend the way of life that is legal in Muslim countries. That is why the Muslim community is pushing to get Sharia Law established in this country so atrocities like this will go unpunished. I find it rather ironic that in their own countries, crimes of rape, adultery and homosexuality are punishable by death. But yet, a family member who disagrees with the tenets of Islam can be beheaded or run over by a Jeep, and with them, it's ok because it's an "Honor Killing."

But just what is an honor killing? According to Wikipedia, "Honor killings are acts of vengeance, usually death, committed by male family members against female family members, who are held to have brought dishonor upon the family. A woman can be targeted by (individuals within) her family for a variety of reasons, including:

refusing to enter into an arranged marriage, being the victim of a sexual assault, seeking a divorce—even from an abusive husband—or (allegedly) committing adultery. The mere perception that a woman has behaved in a way that "dishonors" her family is sufficient to trigger an attack on her life."[2]

And yet, Muslims in this country are trying to get Sharia Law, where women have basically no rights whatsoever, enacted so they can have their "right" to "legal murder." Theodore Roosevelt once said, "No man is above the law and no man is below it: nor do we ask any man's permission when we ask him to obey it." The attitude of this writer is that if Muslims don't like the laws that we have here in the United States of America, and if they don't want to obey the laws that we have, they can go back to where they came from and live under their own barbaric laws at home.

Hate crimes against Christians are perpetrated by Muslims all over the world and the media remains silent on this. According to ReligionofPeace.com, as of this writing, there have been forty-five attacks on Christians by radical Muslims in 2016 alone.

Just to name a few: On January 27, 2016, in Chibok, Nigeria, suicide bombers sent shrapnel through a vegetable market in a Christian town, killing 16 people and injuring 32.

On January 29, 2016, in Adamawa, Nigeria, A young suicide bomber detonated at a busy market near a church, killing 10 and injuring 28.

On January 31, 2016, in Kaisari, Kenya, militant Muslims raided a Christian village and killed 4 innocent people and injured 1, one of whom was beheaded and another burned inside his home.

On February 24, 2016, in Agatu, Nigeria, Radical Islamic mercenaries swept through a series of Christian villages and slaughtered over 300 hundred people, including pregnant women and children.

On March 4, 2016, in Aden, Yemen, militant Muslims stormed a

---

[2] Merriam Webster Online Dictionary 2016

Catholic retirement home and murdered 16 people, including 4 nuns and the elderly residents.

On March 13, 2016, in Bassam, Ivory Coast, al-Qaeda gunmen assaulted a hotel and murdered anyone who refused to praise Allah with them. The eighteen killed included a 5-year-old Christian who was cut down while praying. 17 others were injured in the attack.

On March 27, 2016, in Lahore, Pakistan, a massive suicide blast targeting Christian families celebrating Easter left 78 dead, half of whom were children, and injured 362 others.

On April 25, 2016 in Enugu, Nigeria, 48 people were reported dead and 60 others were injured after Muslim terrorists attacked their village, hacking, shooting, and burning their homes and church.

On April 30, 2016 in Dadawa, Nigeria, A man and his daughter were burnt alive in their church by Boko Haram.

On May 3, 2016, in Beni, Democratic Republic of the Congo, Allied Democratic Force Islamists hacked and slashed thirty-four Christian villagers to death in their own homes, including eight women and four children.

On July 26, 2016 in Saint-Etienne-du-Rouvray, France, Muslim radicals took hostages at a church and slit the throat of an 84-year-old priest.

The above attacks are not all that were listed on their website, but one can see how many of these attacks are directed at Christians.

They have the audacity to want to erect a Mosque on the site of "Ground Zero" and rub our noses in the murder that they committed in the name of Allah and Jihad, yet they refuse to allow churches to be built in Muslim countries. Pastors; you had better start addressing this issue without using any form of "Hate" speech.

Election Issues

Just before the last election in 2012, my church, and I'm assuming that most other churches did also, received a letter from a group called Americans United for Separation of Church and State. The letter was signed by "The Reverend" Barry Lynn, who is the executive director of the organization." In the letter, "The Reverend" Lynn stated that "Any activity designed to influence the outcome of a partisan election can be construed as intervention. If the IRS determines that your house of worship has engaged in unlawful intervention, it can revoke the institution's tax-exempt status or levy significant fines on the house of worship or its leaders." He goes on to say that churches are to be "wary of so-called 'voter guides.' Such guides are often thinly veiled partisan materials. If the IRS finds that a violation has occurred, it may be the house of worship, not the organization that produced the guide, which is penalized." He states in his letter that all houses of worship are to be "non-partisan" entities. However, his letter reeked with partisanship, especially the part about the voter guides. As I have always stated, the only thing that liberal politicians are afraid of is the truth. Although I particularly didn't endorse a political candidate (from the pulpit), I did preach the issues and let the people decide on their own. If any pastors were intimidated by a letter such as this, shame on them. I find it ironic that Jeremiah Wright's church did not lose its tax-exempt status when Reverend Wright compared Barack Obama to Jesus Christ from his very own pulpit.

For a pastor to tell anyone in their congregation to vote for a particular candidate simply because of his or her skin color, even if his policies go against the Word of God, or if you can't vote for him, to just stay home, is a violation of Godly trust. God and God's Word is supposed to come first. A person's skin color should have no bearing on whether or not we vote for him or her. Our votes should be based on the values the person brings to the office.

In 2012, LifeWay researchers found that 90% of pastors in the United States believe that a pastor should not preach politics from the pulpit. Does this mean that they should not preach the issues of an upcoming election from the pulpit? This was a major factor in the way the election results turned out. However, I also believe that God, in His infinite wisdom, has let this happen to our country because that is what the people wanted.

In 2014, George Barna, research expert and founder of The

Barna Group, shared with American Family Radio's 'Today's Issues' about new information he compiled at American Culture and Faith Institute over the last two years, gauging where theologically conservative pastors are at politically.

"'What we're finding is that when we ask them about all the key issues of the day, [90 percent of them are] telling us, 'Yes, the Bible speaks to every one of these issues.' Then we ask them: Well, are you teaching your people what the Bible says about those issues? Then the numbers drop...to less than 10 percent of pastors who say they will speak to it."

Every time I read and study the Book of Revelation, it's like reading the morning newspaper. Jesus is coming soon, so be ready.

Too many people will also listen to the human puppets in Hollywood who endorse a certain candidate and take it as gospel. "Well, if this 'actor' or 'actress' endorses this person, then I guess I'll vote for him or her!" These people live in a dream world and cannot be trusted. Just remember; an actor or actress is merely someone who reads words that someone else wrote and got rich doing it. Pray about who to vote for, let God be your "voter guide" and don't be misled by people who, in essence, hate Christianity.

I truly believe that Christians who prayed, fasted and got out and voted during this last election were seen by God as sincere in their beliefs and God had intervened in the election process and has given this country and Christians another chance. I hope we take advantage of the reprieve that God has given this country.

Fear of Sharing Ones Faith

I saved this for the last item in this chapter for a reason. In 1998, Bill Bright did a survey of Christians all over the world and found that ninety-eight percent of all Christians did not witness regularly to others about Jesus Christ. This is a sad figure to be sure. There are a number of reasons for this, none of which are valid. Let's discuss the major reasons that people don't witness to others.

The major reason people don't witness is that they're afraid that people will think of them as some sort of religious zealot or "Bible thumper." Most of these types of people are closet Christians. If they would only read the Bible and see what commands Jesus gave to the disciples when he sent them out to proclaim His word. He told them in Matthew 10:14 *"And whosoever shall not receive you, nor hear your words, when ye depart out of that house or city, shake off the dust of your feet."* What these people fail to realize is that Jesus was telling us that we were not always going to be successful in winning souls to Christ. But if you truly witness to someone and they reject the Word of God, then we are released from the responsibility of that person's blood being on our hands. I'm not saying to just completely give up, but at least we have done what we have been commanded to do. We have this mindset that we are supposed to win everyone to Christ, but in reality, we are supposed to witness to everyone. The decision to accept or reject what we say is ultimately up to them. Rejection happens. It's a fact of life and there is nothing you or I can do about it except pray for that person. But it should not deter us from our duties as Christians. Leon H. Ellis wrote a song called, *Win the Lost at Any Cost*. How true those words are. How we look in the eyes of others fades quickly when we compare it to how we look in the eyes of God. People sometimes use the excuse, "Well, you know the old saying, 'You can lead a horse to water but you can't make them drink'." Quite frankly, it's not your job to make them drink; it's your job to make them thirsty. When they see how happy and at peace you are, they will thirst for the water of life just like you did. No matter what you may think, there are still people out in the highways and byways who are truly longing for something to ease their troubled minds and hearts. They would be genuinely interested in hearing about the Lord Jesus Christ and His love for them. I have talked to people who have been saved for 30, 40, and even 50 years. When I ask them how many people they have led to Christ, many of them just drop their heads and say, "None." What a tragic testimony! To think of being saved that long, daily talking to people who were unsaved; limitless opportunities wasted. Why? Because they were afraid of what that person might think about them if they shared their faith.

Curtis Hutson would go out on Interstate 85 in Georgia and take a gas can with him. He would find a stranded motorist, fill their car up from the gas can and witness to them. He led 18 people to the Lord this way and one of the men in his church left a pick-up truck to the church in his will so they would always have a vehicle in which to go witnessing.

Some folks plead ignorance when it comes to witnessing. They are afraid that someone will ask them a question they can't answer. They are afraid that they will appear to be stupid or unversed in the ideals of Christianity. This should never be a deterrent. I never go out witnessing until I have prayed and asked God to guide me to the people He would have me to talk to about the Lord that particular day. If someone should ask a question to which you don't know the answer, be honest about it and tell them you don't know. It's much better to be honest about it then to try to do a tap dance on two left feet. There is absolutely nothing wrong with telling someone you don't know, but always tell them you will get the answer and get back to them. I found that when I was witnessing as a new Christian that God had always given me answers I never knew I had until the questions were asked. This comes from faithful Bible study and fervent prayer before going out soul winning.

The Answer to Fear

What most Christians fail to realize is that they can turn their fearfulness into fruitfulness. There is nothing more valuable to a church than a fruitful Christian. By fruitfulness, I don't merely mean winning souls. A fruitful Christian is a laboring Christian. One who works diligently for the church whether it is preaching, visitation, soul winning, cleaning the church or cutting the grass or preparing meals, etc; whatever God has placed on your heart to do. I know people whose only job was to hand out bulletins and shake hands with people as they came into church. The important part was that they were faithful in their duty and if there is one thing that I have learned that God blesses immensely, it's faithfulness. As long as we

Dr. Dale I. Morgan

remember that there are no unimportant jobs in the church and that no one is more important than any other person, then we'll all get along better and we will overcome our fears and become fruitful. Not just in our spiritual lives, but in our family lives also.

Chapter 2
APATHY

Apathy is another serious malady that affects and infects Christians throughout the world. It is defined as a lack of interest or concern, especially regarding matters of general importance or appeal; indifference.[3]

It's as if their mindset is, "Well, if it can't hold my attention for more than sixty seconds, it must not be important."

Apathy in Church Attendance

As I stated in the introduction of this book, we are commanded to assemble together. Paul stated in Hebrews 10:25, "*Not forsaking the assembling of ourselves together, as the manner of some is; but exhorting one another; and so much the more, as ye see the day approaching.*" I cannot begin to tell you how frustrating it is for a pastor to look out on his congregation week after week, month after month and year after year, and not be able to see someone sitting in church two weeks in a row. A recent Gallup Poll showed that 56% of Americans said that religion was very important in their lives. It goes on to say that only about 56% of all church members attend church almost every Sunday.

---

[3]   Merriam Webster Online Dictionary 2016

When you look at Hebrews 10:25, you will notice that the word *forsake*, it's the Greek word ἐγκαταλείπω, (enkataleipō) which has the idea of *deserting or leaving behind*.[1] I picture the writer of Hebrews preaching this passage of Scripture and saying, "Let's not forsake the church. Let's not desert our brothers and sisters in Christ." And then I see him giving a stern, squinty-eyed look, staring directly into the eyes of some of the church members and then saying, "Like some of you are in the habit of doing!" This is a strong rebuke that says we are to be faithful in our church membership and attendance. How do we expect to be victorious in our daily Christian lives if we don't attend church on a regular basis? It goes on to say that we are to **exhort one another.** In the world we live in today, who needs more encouragement than Christians? We are being characterized as fanatics, lunatics, Bible thumpers, radicals and idiots. If you look at what the Hollywood crowd thinks of us, you would see that every time a Christian is portrayed in a sitcom or movie, they always make the Christian out to be some kind of idiot. They viciously attack Christianity because Christianity virtually condemns the very lifestyle they are living. If they truly accept Christ as Lord and Savior, they know that they will have to alter their lifestyle, which in turn would cost them millions upon millions of dollars in revenue. They absolutely will not bite the hand that feeds them, hence, the attacks on Christianity. Not only that, but with people watching the trash and filth that comes out of Hollywood, that's exactly the impression that most unsaved and unchurched people have of Christians. If reports are correct, dozens of Hollywood stars nude photos were "leaked" to the internet and now they are upset as to who would do such a thing. Had they not taken the photos in the first place, we would not even be having this discussion. Hypocrites!

We need to stay strong in our faith and the only way we can do that is to be faithful in our church attendance, encouraging and being encouraged. Faithful church attendance is a must!

Some might say, "Well, the Bible doesn't say that we have to go to church Sunday morning, Sunday evening and Wednesday evening." You are absolutely correct. It doesn't "directly" say that.

But when the church doors are open, why wouldn't you want to be there? The average time that it takes to be in church on a Sunday morning is about two and a half hours. On Sunday night it takes about an hour of ones time. Wednesday evening is about the same. So we are talking about four and a half hours per week for church attendance. That is four and a half hours out of one hundred twelve waking hours per week. It still leaves one hundred seven and a half of waking hours to do whatever else you have to do. I think that is a small price to pay for what Jesus Christ did for all of us, don't you? Someone once said, "You can tell how popular the church is by who comes on Sunday Morning; you can tell how popular the pastor is by who comes on Sunday night, and you can tell how popular Jesus is by who comes on Wednesday night. We sit in church and grumble and moan when the preacher goes past 12 o'clock. If you're a Baptist like me, you're probably saying to yourself, "I wish he'd shut up. The Methodists are going to be first in line at the buffet restaurant and there won't be anything left for us to eat."

I've been in churches where you couldn't get people to come out for a Wednesday evening Bible study, but, if you planned a picnic, or a fishing, bowling, or a golf outing, they will come out of the woodwork in order to get there. We surely don't want to miss out on the fun, but let's skip the Bible study because it's not nearly as much fun as the other things we do.

Revivals seem to be another "thorn in the flesh" for most Christians. I find it unfathomable that we can have some of the greatest preachers in the world in the pulpit for a revival meeting and you can't fill the church on one single night. In the same vein, however, if a church has a singing group or gospel program that "entertains", you have to put extra chairs in the aisles for everyone to sit down. Christian, if you would rather be entertained than preached to, you need to get right with God. Now, don't get me wrong; I'm all for having singing groups in churches. I enjoy them just as much as the next person. But I also know that I need to be preached to a lot more than I need to be sung to, and it's important to support the revivals or any other preaching of the Gospel in the church.

Apathy in Soul Winning

I find it unconscionable to think that all the cult religions out there today are more dedicated to getting people in their houses of worship than we are such as the Mormons, Jehovah's Witnesses, and even the Satanic cults, which by the way are recruiting teenagers by the hundreds. Whether one knows it or not, soul winning is the most important duty of any Christian.

I mentioned in the previous chapter about Fear of Sharing One's Faith. There is a huge difference in being afraid to do something and just not wanting to do it. Every day, we come in contact with people who we work with, go to school with, go hunting and fishing with, play golf with and even go shopping with, and never one time mention Jesus Christ to them. Contrary to popular belief, it's not just the pastor's job to try and win people to Christ. If you're saved, it's your job also.

We have a great responsibility to share the gospel to all with whom we come in contact. God told Ezekiel in Ezekiel 3:18, *When I say unto the wicked, Thou shalt surely die; and thou givest him not warning, nor speakest to warn the wicked from his wicked way, to save his life; the same wicked man shall die in his iniquity; but his blood will I require at thine hand.* How would you feel someday when the lost are being judged at the Great White Throne Judgment and someone you know, before being cast into an everlasting hell, looked you in the eye and said, "Why didn't you tell me?" That person's blood will be on your hands because you failed to tell them about the saving blood of Jesus Christ. Every Christian in every country and in every generation is guilty of this terrible sin. Aren't you glad someone told you about Jesus Christ and His sacrificial death on the cross? Think of how glad someone else will be when you tell them about Jesus and His love for them. We must not take our Godly responsibilities lightly. If you truly love the Lord Jesus Christ, then you'll love what He loves. *"For God so loved the world. . ."* How many times has God laid a burden on your heart for a particular individual and you didn't follow through on it?

An easy way to remedy that problem is that if you know someone and you don't know whether that person is saved or not, just ask them if they are saved. How many of our family members are lost, undone, dying and going to hell because we didn't say anything to them? Some people say that it's hard to witness to family, but I think it's easier, because you know how they will react when confronted. At the very least, they should be the easiest ones to talk to about Jesus.

One more thing; one should never witness to anyone without first praying and asking God to guide your words and your wisdom. Prayer is the best weapon a Christian has and we should always utilize it to the fullest. If you do this, I truly believe with all my heart that you will find soul winning a joy instead of a burden.

Apathy in Our Worship of God

My first question in this segment to the Christian is "Do you take your bible to church with you when you attend services?" If the pastor is preaching and you don't follow along with your bible, how do you know he's preaching the truth of what God's Word says? I see people every Sunday without a bible, staring into space because they're not the least bit interested in learning more about God's Word or His plan for their lives.

Some churches have gotten rid of having Sunday school altogether. This is a complete travesty in modern day churches. If the truth was known, a good Sunday school program enlightens more Christians than one would think. But nowadays, it's much too inconvenient to have to go to Sunday school and also attend the morning worship service. After all, the thinking is, "That's just too much to expect of me." The apathy comes in with the question of "How interested are you in learning the things of God." It only goes to prove that God does not have preeminence in your life if you have no desire to learn about Him and to seek His ways for your life.

Another area where apathy plays a big part in our worship of God is not being mission minded. Missions should be one of the most important aspects of any bible believing, bible preaching church.

Adrian Rogers once said, "Any church that doesn't have a missions program is a mission field in itself." How true those words are today. Most denominations pay thousands of dollars, or millions of dollars each year to their respective conventions, councils, and presbyteries to support the mission programs of that part particular denomination. I have to inject here that if you don't know who your money is going to support, whether it is just someone who says he or she is called to be a missionary, and you don't know what their beliefs are, can you feel comfortable supporting them? Each church should have its own mission program and support its own missionaries, regardless of the hierarchies paid missionaries. My church, albeit a small to medium sized church, broke with the convention on this issue and now supports its own missionaries in Nigeria, India and China. All these people are known by our church. The missionaries from Nigeria have visited my church and my wife and I have visited their work in Ogbomosho Nigeria. These people in Nigeria are so very hungry for the Word of God. I preached at their Homecoming Service and the building was packed. So much so that the windows were opened and people were listening to the message through the open windows. As a result, 90 people came to a saving knowledge of Jesus Christ that day. Such a blessing that day was. I'll never forget it. They also have an orphanage there where they raise all the children in the nurture and admonition of the Lord. Our missionaries in India have been supported by us for almost 4 years now and our church has purchased land for them and they are in the process of building a church and a bible college in Melukavumattom, India in Kerala state. My wife and I have also visited this work and we know the doctrine of the pastor and his people. They are totally on fire for God. We have a missionary in China who visits our church every time he returns to the United States on furlough. The last time he was here, we had several in our church who worked very hard raising money for him. As our southern heritage would have it, our church sold boiled peanuts and raised over a thousand dollars for his work. He was almost in tears.

What I'm trying to say here is this; whether you have a large church or a small church, become personally involved in missions. God will bless everything you do to bring His Word to people all around the world.

Apathy in honoring and respecting the House of God

Let us first talk about the House of God itself. I will take time to explain the purpose of the church in the next chapter but I want to make it perfectly clear that the House of God is exactly that; The House of God. It seems now that we have to have "catch phrases" for God's House now. Phrases like, "The Church for People Who Don't like Church." "The Church Where It's Ok to Not Be Ok." Whatever happened to "So and So Baptist Church" or "So and So Methodist Church" or "Presbyterian" or whoever? At least with the denominational name, people will have some idea as to what kind of doctrine the church has. Are they ashamed of the doctrine? Why even have a church if you're not going to try to help people get their lives straightened out? I get so sick of "Gimmicks in the name of God" that it makes me want to throw up. Preachers, if you're not going to preach God's Word, meaning that you should be preaching that people are lost and dying in their sins, preaching that if they don't repent of their sins and ask God to save them that they're going to die and spend an eternity in hell, then you, my friends, are poor excuses for preachers. Get rid of the gimmicks, get rid of the showmanship, get rid of the bells and whistles and start doing what God expects of all His preachers, and that is preaching the Word.

The reason we're not getting people saved anymore is because these phony baloney pastors are afraid that if they insult someone they'll lose money. Hear me on this and hear me well; God's Word wasn't popular during Jesus' time, and it's not popular now. But that didn't stop Jesus nor His disciples from preaching the truth. As a matter of fact, all of them except for John, died martyr's deaths for being true to God's Word.

In today's culture it seems as if it is such an inconvenience to attend church, and when and if we do decide to attend services, we do so at the expense of honoring God's House in several areas.

Years ago, people used to dress up for church. The ladies would wear dresses and the men would wear a suit and tie. I remember a painting by Norman Rockwell entitled "Sunday Morning" of a man sitting in an easy chair in his bathrobe and pajamas with the Sunday paper scattered all over the floor, smoking a cigarette. His wife and children were walking out the door single file all dressed up going to church with Bibles in their hands. The wife had a look on her face that said, "If you're not going to take the lead in taking our children to church, then I will." The sheepish look on the man's face was priceless.

Today, people dress like they are going to a beach party instead of church. They come into the sanctuary on Sunday morning wearing shorts, flip-flops, and a shirt that gives the impression that they are saying, "Hey, I'm a tourist in Hawaii." Pastors are just as much to blame for this "phenomena" as the rest of the church. I believe that a pastor should set the example for dress codes in the church and if the pastor dresses like he's going to a "come as you are" party, then it will naturally trickle down to the rest of the congregation. I know of a pastor in Florida who got in the pulpit on Sunday morning wearing nothing but blue jeans and a t-shirt that said, "Jesus! What a Man!" This shows a total disrespect for our Lord and Savior. He is God in the flesh and should be honored as such.

I know that many people will be offended by what I say here about the way they dress when they come to church, especially some pastors. They will say, "Well, you just don't understand. After all, we've come a long way baby." No! Because when you say you've come a long way, it implies that you have arrived at some destination. What you have really done is "GONE" a long way; meaning that you have gotten farther away from where you started. It looks as if, when we are sitting in church, that we are sitting in someone's back yard at a neighborhood barbeque instead of a preaching service. There doesn't seem to be much modesty in either male or female attire anymore. At the risk of sounding old-fashioned, I would like to reiterate that we need to remember where we are and why we are there. I don't think having a small amount of decency is asking too much for anyone. But nowadays, we have this "Don't tell me what to do" attitude and whiney little people get offended at the least little things. All I'm saying is that we need to have more pride in the house of God and more pride in ourselves. Casual dress codes lead to casual worship and when it comes to worshiping God, it should have our full effort; not just a casual, nonchalant, "Well, at least I tried" attitude.

I feel that I would be not completely thorough on the matter of clothing if I didn't mention the other extreme. There are those who feel that a person is "worldly" if a woman wears make-up, jewelry and/or slacks. They feel that a pastor is "worldly" if he preaches in anything other than a white shirt, or if he has facial hair. I have to compare these to the very ones who crucified Jesus Christ. These modern day, man-made pharisaical ideas are no different than the Pharisees of Jesus time nit picking everything He and His disciples did. Some of these pastors will not even go to preach in any church who doesn't adhere to their "code." They seem to be in their own little world placing judgment on others just like Caiaphas did with Jesus before he was taken before Pilate.

Church music is another area of concern, and to some degree, consternation. Too many churches of late have done away with the old hymns they used to sing and replaced them with bands, synthesizers, drums and the like. Modern church music makes one feel like they're at a rock concert instead of being in the house of God. One of the biggest oxymoron's in the world is the phrase "Christian Rock." The music sounds the same as worldly rock music and most of the musicians don't look any different either. It's like saying "Christian Beer" or "Christian Cigarettes." There's no such thing. ***Come out from among them and be ye separate**" said Paul. We're not supposed to look like the world and we're not supposed to act like the world. Churches used to have song leaders, but now they have "Worship Leaders" as they now call them. They will get up there and try to "pump up" the crowd and create excitement and call it "spirituality." Most of the modern day "worship" songs now are just hastily strung together words that someone has written in order to make a name for oneself. Then we have what this author calls the "7/11" songs. Songs that have 7 verses and they sing each verse 11 times. Many churches today start their services off what I call "Rock Concert Style. They have a great light show, the "worship leader" getting everyone up to the highest crescendo he possibly can, and then all of a sudden, here comes the pastor coming on stage through the lights and the fog.

Not many songs are written that concern the blood, the sacrifice and the Cross of Christ anymore. In my church we sing the old hymns about ninety-nine percent of the time. As a matter of fact, the Presbyterian (USA), Episcopal, Disciples, United Church of Canada, and United Church of Christ hymnals have now deleted songs about the blood atonement. Harry Emerson Fosdick, (1878-1969), a Presbyterian pastor in New York City in the early 1900's once said that the idea of Jesus' death on a Cross as a substitution for the sins of others was a slaughterhouse religion. However, the shed blood of Jesus Christ IS the Gospel and nothing can change that.

Not only that, but the New Methodist Hymnal of 1989 has become so "Politically Correct" it is almost to the point of sickening. Songs like "His power and His love," were changed to "God's power and God's love." They apparently don't look at God in the "masculine" form anymore lest we insult the feminists. *"Sons of men and angels say Alleluia"* is now *"Earth and heaven in chorus say Alleluia."* To top the whole thing off, and I have to laugh about this or I'd probably cry, in the hymn *"Nothing But the Blood of Jesus,"* the word "bright" was substituted for "white" in the verse "O precious is the flow, that makes me white as snow."

Which brings me to my next point. The preaching of God's Holy Word, or should I say, "The Lack Thereof." Most of today's preaching in the New Age and Emergent Churches is more for show than it is for Jesus Christ. People are so enamored with the light shows, the pep talks and the impressive way the pastor conducts himself, that they're not interested in hearing the true Word of God. The pastor will come out in blue jeans and a T-shirt to be "one of ya'll" so to speak! Some preach on the blood atonement but most are, quite frankly, in it for the money. The more people you have in your church, it stands to reason that the more money you're going to bring in. I have nothing against large churches, however when a church is so large that they have to have movie screens on either side of the pulpit just to see the pastor, it all of a sudden becomes very impersonal. There is no way a pastor can relate to all the people in his church that way. Then he has to rely on his staff members to do counseling, visitation and the like. Unless he has the deepest trust in the world in these people, or staff and they call them now, I would be very concerned that my people were being well taken care of and that their needs were being met.

Many churches have done away with the old fashioned altar altogether. Some very rarely, if ever, give altar calls. Whatever happened to the old fashioned "mourners benches" they used to have in churches. These were pews, generally in the front of churches, where repentant people could come and cry because of their sins, or some were coming to receive Christ as their savior. I don't know of any church that has this anymore. There may be some, but I've not heard of any. It's a shame that people aren't broken by their sin anymore. Altar calls used to be the climax of a worship service and people would pour down the aisles to get their lives right with God. However, pride has taken away all that now. The attitude is something like, "Well, if I go forward to the altar, so and so will wonder what I've been up to and we can't have anyone knowing that I sinned this past week." If the truth be known, every beating heart in the congregation had sinned the previous week and they're thinking the very same thing. God told the Israelites to "*humble themselves.*" The very same command comes to us also as children of God. When was the last time you saw someone run down the aisle and fall on their knees at the altar broken hearted because of their sin? Most would probably answer "never!" That is the shame of the Christian life today. Unconfessed sin builds a wall between the Christian and God and the only means of tearing down that wall is to confess one's sin. Most people today aren't sorry that they sinned; they're sorry that they got caught sinning.

Did you ever stop to think that maybe if you went to the altar, it would encourage someone else to go? The problem with so many Christians today is the "Me" syndrome. What will they say about "Me?" What will they think about "Me?" How is it going to affect "Me?" What's in it for "Me?" My question is, "What does God think about "Me?" Christians are not supposed to be a selfish lot. They're supposed to be considerate of others. Maybe you holding back going to the altar is affecting someone else. We would do well to be an example for others whose faith isn't as strong as ours. It's also true that the altar is a good place to thank God for the things He has done for you in the past week. Did you get a blessing from God? Did you thank Him for it? Why not?

Pastors, I'm taking time to mention to you here to not forsake the giving of altar calls, not just for salvation, but for repenting of sins, and for those to lay their burdens on the altar and to let God handle them. You do a great injustice by not giving folks the chance to repent, unload burdens and to thank God. To not have an altar call is to deny people the opportunity to kneel in front of Almighty God and get saved, to kneel and confess their sins, to kneel before God and praise Him for a blessing they received or to pray for a lost loved one. We as pastors need to get back to the basics and that means to stop putting on a "Show for Dough" and being true to the Word of God.

This next point may invoke the wrath of the reader, however I feel I would be remiss if I don't mention it, especially from a Christian standpoint. I'm taking about tattoos! Never in my life time have I seen such a surge of a fad like the marking up of one's body. Although the Bible does not directly address it in the New Testament, Leviticus 19:28 says, *Ye shall not make any cuttings in your flesh for the dead, nor print any marks upon you: I am the LORD.* Although the Lord was talking about doing this in honoring pagan gods, it still is something we should look at today.

People today have taken this practice to extreme levels. I saw a picture of one man who was tattooed from the very top of his head to the bottom of his feet. To be very honest, he reminded me of a little pet turtle I had when I was a child that I kept in an aquarium.

Some have their entire arms and legs tattooed in the name of "art," and are very proud of how they look. However, one eventually grows old and the ink will fade, the skin will sag, and an eagle on the chest eventually grows into a buzzard on the belly. I feel that the reason people cover their bodies with all these tattoos is because no one has told them how foolish they look. Oh, ok, call me a prude, but it's true. The only place you ever saw folks like this a few years ago was in a freak show at a county fair.

It is not addressed in the New Testament, but Paul tells us in 1 Corinthians 6:19, *What? know ye not that your body is the temple of the Holy Ghost which is in you, which ye have of God, and ye are not your own?* If you claim the name of Christ, we should be very careful how we treat His temple. We are all created by God and we don't need to be altering it to suit what is popular in the world. I know that some are saying, "Well, what about women wearing make-up?" Make-up is not a permanent thing.

I once asked a man who I saw in a local Walmart one time who had his right arm completely tattooed if that was expensive. He stated to me, "It is if you get a good one because it is 'forever.' This one cost me $2,200.00." I thought to myself, "My, what a waste of money."

The excuse is, "Well, everyone is doing it. We need to fit in." However, we are told by the Apostle Paul in 2 Corinthians 6:17 *Wherefore come out from among them, and be ye separate, saith the Lord, and touch not the unclean thing; and I will receive you.* Before anyone makes the accusation that I'm "judging" people, let me remind you of one important thing. The Bible teaches that we are "in" the world, however we are not to be "of" the world. We are to "separate" ourselves from the things of the world. We are a called out assembly, and we are to be recognized as such. Separation from the things of this world will make Christians more "recognizable" to other lost people, which is exactly what is supposed to happen. Someone once said, "If you were accused of being a Christian, would there be enough evidence to convict you?"

Another area of concern as far as not honoring God's house is an issue that is a particular sore spot with this writer; cell phones.

Nothing angers me more than to have a cell phone go off during a church service; whether it is during the song service or the preaching service. It shows a total lack of respect for not only the House of God and the pastor, but for others around you who have come to worship. One of the first things we say in our announcements at our church is, "Please turn all cell phones off!" And, yes, we had to do it for a reason. It was totally disrupting to the service and we had to put a stop to it.

Texting is another problem with the cell phone issue. It is totally rude and disrespectful to sit in church and be totally oblivious to what the pastor is saying because someone is texting someone else during the preaching of God's Word. I have been in churches where an entire service was spent by someone texting on their cell phone. Since the innovation of the Smart Phone, have you ever noticed that if someone is holding a "smart phone," you cannot hold someone's attention in a conversation for any length of time at all? Oh, they'll be listening to you, but for sure, every few seconds or so, they will be checking their phone to see what has come up on their screen. It seems as if one's entire life revolves around that little piece of technology in their hand. What kind of a revival would we have in this country if people would be as adamant about Jesus Christ and their bibles as they are about their cell phones?

We have become too lax in our enthusiasm for worship. I know of several churches who cancelled services so they could show the Super Bowl on television. I also personally know of a church that has cancelled one Sunday evening service per month so they can show a movie. "Oh, this is how we reach out to people" some may say. It seems that Hollywood and the NFL are more important than the Holy Spirit and that, somehow, God will be cheering for whoever is playing. The attitude that God thinks it is alright to interrupt a service for a movie or an athletic event is preposterous. I truly wonder if they passed out popcorn and refreshments in the sanctuary. You can be sure that there was a lot of cheering going on that night during the Super Bowl. But the church was probably as quiet as a morgue when the pastor was preaching the following Sunday. Would to God that they had the kind of enthusiasm and excitement for the Lord Jesus Christ that they had as they watched the Super Bowl that night. God help them when they have to answer for things like that. Christian, hear me on this: You don't miss church to watch a football game, and you don't cancel a church service to watch a movie. Any thing you put before God becomes a god in itself, and God Himself said in Exodus 34:14, *"For thou shalt worship no other god: for the LORD, whose name is Jealous, is a jealous God."*

There are indeed, preachers going from one extreme to another.

We've also seen churches making a mockery of the Ordinance of Baptism. A "church" recently installed a waterslide in order to "mass baptize" unsuspecting people. The people were told that it was a "New Balcony Entrance" and were pushed down the slide into the water. The church had hired auctioneers to stand along the sides of the slide and speedily utter the phrase, "I baptize you in the name of the Father, Son, and Holy Spirit" as the unsuspecting congregants whooshed by into the pool below. The creative pastor of the "church" said the auctioneers were there to speak that phrase, "Otherwise we can't count it." My question is, "Were any of these people saved?" The bible teaches salvation before baptism. It's part of the "anything to draw a crowd" mentality that so many people are falling for these days.

Apathy in Giving to the Lord's Work

Tithing, giving, stewardship, or whatever you wish to call it, is at an all time low in churches today. In the most recent Barna Poll that I could find, in 2007, among all born again adults, only 9% contributed one-tenth or more of their income to the church. The survey went on to say that only 76% of all born again adults gave any money at all to the church. Although the tithe (or the tenth part) is the basis on which people should give, the Apostle Paul also states in 1 Corinthians 16:2 that we should give *"as God hath prospered him."* I understand that some people have a hard time making ends meet. But others of us have been blessed over and above what we expected in our lives and thus, should give over and above what your "tithe" or tenth part happens to be. Some make the mistake of calling the tithe a gift. This is far from the truth. The tithe is what already belongs to God and we should return it to Him. It is not a "gift" as such until it exceeds the amount of the tithe. An example of this is if you make $1,000.00 per week and you give the church $101.00, you have paid your tithe and given God a $1.00 gift. I'm sorry to have burst some bubbles of pride here, but the truth is the truth and most people haven't really been giving as much of a gift to the Lord's work as they thought they were giving.

We should note here that giving is a very personal matter between the individual and God. I preach a message on tithing about once or twice a year. It seems that people who are not giving are offended that pastors would preach on a matter such as this if, as I stated, giving is a personal matter between the individual and God. I have made it a practice in my ministry that I do not want to know who tithes faithfully and who doesn't. Although I expect my deacons and Sunday school teachers, and anyone else who holds a position in the church to faithfully tithe, I don't ever go to the treasurer and ask who tithes and who doesn't. My reason for this is that I don't want anyone to say, "You know I don't tithe and you were talking about me in that sermon on tithing." I heard an old expression one time that says, "If you throw a rock in amongst a pack of dogs, the one that squeals the loudest is the one that got hit." We should all read and heed the story of the widow's mites in Mark 12:41-44. Yes, it is a story of giving, but it goes farther than that. What you are saying when you give "sacrificially" is that you are putting all your trust in God to supply all of your needs, just as this widow did.

I would ask the reader today, "How much trust do you have that God will supply all your needs?" If you answer in the affirmative, then I submit that it is time to put your money where your mouth is and start trusting God with tithes and offerings. Don't just tell God how much you trust Him; show God how much you trust Him and especially show Him how much you love Him. He stated in Malachi chapter 3 and verse 10, "***Bring ye all the tithes into the storehouse, that*** *there may be meat in mine house, and prove me now herewith, saith the LORD of hosts, if I will not open you the windows of heaven, and pour you out a blessing, that there shall not be room enough to receive it.*" God has promised each and every one a blessing so abundant, that "*there shall not be room enough to receive it.*" So, if you trust God, and you trust God to follow through on His promises, shouldn't you start giving back to God what you owe Him?

Apathy in One's Prayer Life

This is the main reason that America is in the dire straits that it is in today. People aren't praying and, even when they do pray, they don't do it as our Lord showed us how it is to be done. The greatest failure among Christians today is the failure to pray. Even if they do pray, most people's prayer life consists of prayers like, "Lord, do this for me!"; "Lord, give me this, or give me that!"; "Lord, heal me or heal so and so!" And then they follow this with a hearty "AMEN!" When the disciples asked Jesus how to pray, He gave them a model prayer in Luke 11:1-4. Most people just go ahead and pray that prayer word-for-word and then they think that they've done what they're supposed to do. This prayer was strictly an example of the "format" of a proper prayer. I suppose that it is alright to repeat it in a group, but when one gets alone, one-on-one with God, this is just the "outline" of how a proper prayer should be.

The prayer starts out, not with "asking", but with worship. "*And he said unto them, When ye pray, say, Our Father which art in heaven, Hallowed be thy name.* The word "*Hallowed*" means to be "Holy, sanctified, or set apart." When worshiping God, nothing should be put in God's place of importance. So, when we are commencing in prayer, the first thing we should do is worship God. God always comes first, not us! Christianity is not about us; it's about God. He always comes first. Then He says, "*Thy kingdom come. Thy will be done, as in heaven, so in earth.*" Adrian Rogers once said that prayer is not about getting our will done in heaven; it's about getting God's will done here on earth. Some people say, "Well, God's will is always done here on earth." Friends, that is just not true. The Bible states in 2 Peter 3:9, *"The Lord is not slack concerning his promise, as some men count slackness; but is longsuffering to us-ward, not willing that any should perish, but that all should come to repentance."* This verse tells us that God's will is, *"that all should come to repentance"* and that is definitely not happening.

Part of the reason for that is that is that His children (Christians) are not praying often enough and in the correct manner. So when we worship God in our prayer, and we ask for His will to be done above our will, then we can go ahead and make our supplications to Him for our needs and requests. In Matthew chapter 6 and verse 11 Jesus first says, *"Give us this day our daily bread."* Notice He doesn't say, "Give us enough bread to last us a lifetime."? If we asked God to supply our needs for the rest of our lives, how often would we call upon Him? We talk to our wives, our husbands, our children, and our co-workers on a daily basis, but we feel it an "inconvenience" to talk to God on a daily basis. Give God as much time as you do anyone else. Indeed, He is deserving of much more than we give Him. Also in Matthew 6 and verse 12, Jesus tells us we need to ask for forgiveness of sins or debts. The Greek word used here is ὀφείλημα (opheilēma) which means "something owed, or a moral fault." (Strong's Greek & Hebrew Dictionary). He says, *"And forgive us our debts, as we forgive our debtors."* Some scholars may argue with me about this but I'm going to put it here anyway. The word *"as"* is the Greek word καί (kai) and can be translated as "even as, or likewise" (Strong's Greek & Hebrew Dictionary). This tells me that we could be asking God to forgive us in the same manner as we are forgiving others. I really don't think that we would like for God to do that. We surely need to be more forgiving towards others. I'm grateful that God is much more forgiving of me than I am of others, and that is an area in which all of us need to work harder.

Once we have presented all these things to God, we are to thank Him for the answers that will come. Whether God answers a prayer in the way we think He should or not, we should thank Him. We tend to pray and say, "Lord, I have this problem and here's what you need to do to solve it." Of course, then when God answers in a way that is not according to the way we thought He should answer, we get upset at God. The problem is that God sees the "big picture" if you will. God always knows what is best for us and will answer in the way that is best for us. Just present it to God and let Him handle it. Many times I have seen people come to the altar and pour their problems out to God. They deposit all their needs on the altar and then, when they are finished, they pick up the problems again and carry them back to their seat. The secret to answered prayer is to leave the problems at the altar and trust God to handle them. A faithless prayer gets little or no results.

The Apostle Paul said in Romans 15:30, *Now I beseech you, brethren, for the Lord Jesus Christ's sake, and for the love of the Spirit, that ye strive together with me in your prayers to God for me;* The word *strive* in the Greek is συναγωνίζομαι, pronounced *synagōnizomai.* It's where we get our word "agonize." So many people don't really think of prayer as "agonizing" but it's that kind of feeling with which we must pray each and every time we pray.

About 3 years ago we had a one year old girl in our church that needed brain surgery. She was scheduled for surgery on a Thursday morning. This was during a revival that was going on at the church. From Sunday night until Wednesday night, at the end of the revival service, all the members of the church formed a circle and held hands and prayed for that dear little girl. We had people all over the state and friends of ours in Nigeria, India and Canada praying for that little girl. It was, indeed, agonizing prayer for her. But God, in His loving way, answered those prayers and the little girl had the surgery on Thursday, and it went so well that they let her come home on Friday and she was back in church on Sunday. We held to the promise in Matthew 18:19-20, where Jesus said, *Again I say unto you, That if two of you shall agree on earth as touching any thing that they shall ask, it shall be done for them of my Father which is in heaven. ²⁰ For where two or three are gathered together in my name, there am I in the midst of them.*

This brings me to another point. In verse twenty of Matthew 18,

Jesus said *For where two or three are gathered together in my name, there am I in the midst of them.* We have this idea that if we just say, "In Jesus name I pray," that God will answer any prayer we pray. Not true. What you are saying when you say, "In Jesus name I pray," is that if Jesus was here on earth at this time, He would pray for that very same thing. I doubt that Jesus would pray for someone to win the lottery, but people pray in Jesus name for that to happen. So be careful what you pray for in the name of Jesus.

So many times I have heard people say, "Well, I've done everything I know of to do. All I can do now is pray." Frankly speaking, you should have been praying at the outset; even before problems arise in our lives. Many times problems come into our lives because of a lack of prayer. Someone once said, "I have no problem that wasn't at first, a prayer problem."

When you pray, you need to get away from all distractions. Any time you read in the Bible where Jesus prayed, you will always find that He got away from everyone and everything. He wanted no distractions whatsoever while talking with His Heavenly Father. In Luke 6:12, the Bible says, *And it came to pass in those days, that he went out into a mountain to pray, and continued all night in prayer to God.* In Luke 22:41 it says, *And he was withdrawn from them about a stone's cast, and kneeled down, and prayed.* And in Matthew 26:36 it says, *Then cometh Jesus with them unto a place called Gethsemane, and saith unto the disciples, Sit ye here, while I go and pray yonder.*

Don't let anything or anybody distract you from the time you spend with God. If you have to lock yourself in the bathroom, go literally into a closet, or go out and sit in your car; whatever it takes to get alone with God, do it. Make an appointed time, everyday, to speak with the One who has all the answers. To commune with Him, to fellowship with Him and to listen to Him. The Bible says, *"Be still and know that I am God."* So when we are finished with our prayer, we need to sit and listen. We need to see if God has a message for us just as we have a message for Him. Don't just say, "Thank you, Lord. Amen" and then just get up and walk away. Give God an opportunity to put something in your head, in your mind or in your heart for that particular day.

One of the greatest men of prayer, George Mueller once said, "I live in the spirit of prayer. I pray as I walk about, when I lie down and when I rise up. And the answers are always coming. Thousands and tens of thousands of times have my prayers been answered. When once I am persuaded that a thing is right and for the glory of God, I go on praying for it until the answer comes. George Mueller never gives up!" (George Mueller 1805-1898).

Chapter 3

IGNORANCE

"Ignorance is bliss." How many times have we heard that expression by English poet Thomas Gray? Some people pride themselves in ignorance, and it seems that some Christians totally revel in it. What is it that Christians are ignorant of and why do they choose to stay that way?

Ignorance of God's Word

I would first of all like to approach the subject of God's Word Itself. When you think about the bible, what comes to mind? Many people think it's just a book about God. I would like to take some time here to explain just exactly what the bible is and the importance of the bible before I get into the reason for the Ignorance of God's Word. It has been called many things by many people, so let's take a close look at the bible.

The bible is not just a book. It is the sacred writings of God preserved through the centuries, although many have tried unsuccessfully to destroy it. 1 Peter 1:24-25 says *24 For all flesh is as grass, and all the glory of man as the flower of grass. The grass withereth, and the flower thereof falleth away: 25 But the word of the Lord endureth for ever. And this is the word which by the gospel is preached unto you.* Jesus also said in Matthew 24:35 *Heaven and earth shall pass away, but my words shall not pass away.* Down through the centuries, man has tried to destroy, disavow and denigrate the Word of God to no avail. It will be alive and well for all eternity.

The bible is broken down into two separate sections. The Old Testament and the New Testament. The word "testament" means "covenant" describing the promises God made to His people. The Old Testament, of which there are 39 books, tells the story of the history of the Jewish people and how God Chose Abraham as their father or patriarch. There are over 330 prophecies in the Old Testament concerning the Lord Jesus Christ that were fulfilled. The New Testament, having 27 books, tells us about the redemption brought about by the sacrificial death on the cross of Calvary of our Lord and Savior Jesus Christ and how God established His Church.

The bible is called the Scripture and the Scriptures. It's called the "Scripture" in Mark 15:28 where it says *And the scripture was fulfilled, which saith, And he was numbered with the transgressors.* In Matthew 22:29 it is used as "Scriptures" and says *Jesus answered and said unto them, Ye do err, not knowing the scriptures, nor the power of God.* The same Greek word is used in both instances which is γραφή (pronounced graphē). The two words mean "Holy Writings." The bible is also called the Word of God which says volumes for the true stance of the bible. All throughout the New Testament this term is used for the bible. In Hebrews 4:12 we find out just how powerful the Word of God is: *For the word of God is quick, and powerful, and sharper than any twoedged sword, piercing even to the dividing asunder of soul and spirit, and of the joints and marrow, and is a discerner of the thoughts and intents of the heart.* Its *"quick"* meaning it's alive. Someone once said, "It's not only a book that you read, but also a book that reads you." How true. It also says *"sharper than any twoedged sword, piercing even to the dividing asunder of soul and spirit, and of the joints and marrow.* "A two edged sword cuts both ways. Many times during my ministry have I found myself preaching to myself. It can cut the audience and it can cut the preacher who is preaching the message. *And is a discerner of the thoughts and intents of the heart.* The Greek word for *discerner* is **κριτικός**, *kritikos*. It's from where we get our word "critic." Men may be critical of one another. Men may be critical of God's Word. But the Word of God is the only critic that matters. Some may be critical of this book. Some may argue that I, myself am being too critical. However, when it comes right down to it, all the criticism of men doesn't amount to a hill of beans. Each of us have to be concerned about what God thinks of our words and deeds and stop relying on what the world thinks of us.

Having described the bible in detail and what it is called, can we rely on it? How do we know that it is, indeed, the true Word of God?

If you take a close look at the bible, we see that in 2 Timothy 3:16, that *All scripture is given by inspiration of God, and is profitable for doctrine, for reproof, for correction, for instruction in righteousness.* The word *inspiration* is *theopneustos*, and means divinely breathed, or God breathed. So the words that these inspired men wrote were "breathed into them" by the spirit of God. When you put this together with 2 Peter 1:20-21 we see this, *"²⁰Knowing this first, that no prophecy of the scripture is of any private interpretation. ²¹ For the prophecy came not in old time by the will of man: but holy men of God spake as they were moved by the Holy Ghost."* This tells us that some mere mortal man didn't just suddenly decide to say, "I think I'll sit down and write a book and see if I can get it put in the bible." No! The bible tells us that ALL scripture is given by inspiration of God. When you stop to think that the bible was written over a period of 1500 years by over 40 men from all different walks of life, written in 3 different languages on three different continents, and yet the truth falls right into place so easily, dear friends, only God can do something like that. With that kind of proof, it would be very difficult for one to try and deny the Godly inspiration of the Word of God.

Although there are many "versions" of the bible on bookshelves today, only one stands out to me, and that is the King James Version. A careful study that I'll not go into in this book, will show the reader that this version (KJV) is the only one that any Christian should be using. Many of the newer "easy to read" versions intentionally leave out scripture, change the wording and take the deity from Jesus Christ. Some even try to disprove miracles. I will be coming out with another book on this subject next.

People try to put the blame for their ignorance of God's Word with the excuse that, "It's too hard to understand." But I don't believe that for a moment. The true reason for the ignorance of God's Word is "The Ignoring of God's Word."

What do I mean by that? Ask yourself these questions: "How much time do I spend each day studying God's Word?" "How much time do I spend each week studying God's Word?" "How much time do I spend each year studying God's Word?" Are you embarrassed yet? According to a recent Gallup Poll, only 37% of all Christians read their Bible once a week. How does one expect to learn anything by reading once a week? No wonder churches have weak Christians. Your faith is weak because you only feed it once per week. If you only ate one meal per week, wouldn't you feel weak and malnourished?

Every Christian should have on their daily schedule time set aside to read God's Word. I'm not talking about a five minute devotional here; I'm talking about 30 minutes or more of real study so you can unwrap the wonders of God's love for you and everyone else. Unfortunately, in the hustle and bustle of our daily routine, the things of God have to take a back seat to everything else and get swept under the rug.

Yes, bible study takes work; it takes time and it takes a lot of self-will, but in the end, it pays with benefits; benefits such as the privilege of standing boldly for Jesus Christ in a chaotic world. In 1 Peter 3:15 we are called to *"sanctify the Lord God in your hearts: and be ready always to give an answer to every man that asketh you a reason of the hope that is in you with meekness and fear."* I know Christians who have been saved for 40 and 50 years and could no more lead a person to Christ than the man in the moon. What a travesty! What this all boils down to is the fact that we, as Christians, are not giving enough study to the Word of God.

I am constantly amazed at the number of people who are completely satisfied to sit in church Sunday after Sunday and let the pastor expound the Word of God and never follow along in their Bibles (if they even brought a Bible to church). How in the world do they know that what the pastor is saying to them is the truth? Paul told Timothy in Second Timothy 2:15, "*Study to shew thyself approved unto God, a workman that needeth not to be ashamed, rightly dividing the word of truth.*" I know that there are some who would argue that this passage pertains to pastors and teachers, and indeed it does. But it also says "*workman*" which, in the Greek is ἐργάτης, *ergatēs*, meaning laborer, fellow laborer, worker, etc. If you are a saved Christian, then God has called you to be a worker or laborer for His cause, and you should study to give correct answers to others who might be interested in hearing more about God and His wonderful salvation.

Let me ask you, the reader, another question. If someone came up to you and said, "Can you tell me what the Bible says about being saved? Can you show me how I can know that I am going to heaven when I die?" What would your answer be to that person? Would you say, "Well, I'm not quite sure. Let me ask my pastor and I will get back to you."? Would you say, "No, I'm sorry, but I just don't know enough about the Bible to tell you. I know that I'm saved, but you'll have to find out for yourself"? Or could you stand tall and proud and say, "Yes, I surely can tell you how to be saved. Let's look at the Bible together and see what it says. I would be happy to show you."?

It is every Christian's duty and obligation to be able to tell someone else how to be saved. You know how you got saved, so be ready with an answer and be able to tell someone else how to be saved. This generation of Christians is much too ignorant concerning the Word of God. If I asked one hundred Christians why they don't study the Bible like they should, I would probably get 99 different excuses. Notice that I didn't' say that I would get "99 different answers." When it comes to studying the Word of God, it is a command and not an option. Any defense for disobedience to the Word of God is an excuse, not an answer.

It is truly unfortunate that many pastors, who claim to know the Word of God, are totally ignorant of what the Scriptures say about salvation and the way to heaven. If there are any liberals reading this book, I'm sure that right about now you are going to say, "Oh no! Here's another right winger preaching that Jesus Christ is the only way to heaven." Well, for once in your life, you are absolutely right on the money. If you believe the Bible, and I do, then you have no other alternative but to believe that Jesus is the only way to heaven. John 14:6 says, *"I am the way, the truth, and the life: no man cometh unto the father but by me."* Very clear, very concise, and yet there are pastors who have trouble dealing with this.

A good example of this is a very prominent and popular television preacher, who sat on national television and was asked the question, "What if you're Jewish or Muslim, and don't accept Christ at all." His answer was a cop-out for Christianity. He said, "You know, I'm very careful about saying who would and wouldn't go to heaven. . . I spent a lot of time in India with my father, and I don't know much about their religion, but I do know that they love God. I've seen their sincerity. I just don't know." The Pharisees were very sincere in their beliefs, and they also loved God, but Jesus called them a generation of vipers. The Apostle Paul himself said about the Jews in Romans chapter 10 and verses 1-3 very plainly, *"Brethren, my heart's desire and prayer to God for Israel is, that they might be saved. ²For I bear them record that they have a zeal of God, but not according to knowledge. For they being ignorant of God's righteousness, and going about to establish their own righteousness, have not submitted themselves unto the righteousness of God.* Paul states that the Jews had *"a zeal"* for God, but they were wrong in their thinking about God. You can be sincere, but still be sincerely wrong. Mr. Osteen is a pastor making millions and millions of dollars every year and doesn't have the courage to stand up and defend what our Lord and Savior said concerning salvation. He's a very dangerous pastor because he gets up there with his expensive suits, cute smile, charismatic personality and sweet soft voice and tells people that "everything is going to be Ok." Everything is not going to be ok unless you get people saved by telling them that they are lost and sinful in God's eyes and to repent of their sins. That's the Bible way. It's not my way, or Osteen's way or anyone else's way; it's God's way.

Ignorance of Who Jesus Christ Really Is

Who is Jesus? Man? Myth? Legend? Just who is Jesus Christ? Some folks think He's just someone we pray to when we're in trouble or if we need something.

If you ask a Jehovah's Witness, they will tell you that Jesus was the first created being of Jehovah God. Jehovah God created Jesus as a divine-like spirit at some point in ancient, pre-creation time. "This means that he was created before all the other spirit sons of God, and that he is the only one who was directly created by God" (*You Can Live Forever in Paradise on Earth [Live] [Brooklyn: Watchtower Bible and Tract Society of New York, 1982], p. 58*). According to the Watchtower Society, before He came to earth, Jesus was known as "the Word" (John 1:3, 10, 14) because He was God's spokesman. He is also identified by Jehovah's Witnesses with Michael the archangel. "Reasonably, then, the archangel Michael is Jesus Christ. So the evidence indicates that the Son of God (Jesus) was known as Michael before he came to earth" (*Reasoning from the Scriptures [Reasoning] [Brooklyn: Watchtower Bible and Tract Society of New York, 1985], p. 218*). They don't believe for one nanosecond that Jesus Christ was God in the flesh.

If you ask a Mormon who Jesus Christ is, they will tell you that Jesus is the first baby born to God in heaven. They also teach that Jesus and Lucifer were brothers in Heaven (*Gospel Through the Ages - 1946 Priesthood Manual by Milton R. Hunter, p. 15*). The Bible says that Jesus created everything that was created and made (John 1:3, Col. 1:16). This includes the Devil since only God was in existence in the beginning. That means Jesus only came into being when he was born in the pre-existence and had to work out his way to becoming a God. Mormonism denies that Jesus was God in the flesh also.

But who is Jesus really?

The bible is very clear on who Jesus is.

He is God. Hebrews 1:8 states specifically, *But unto the Son he saith, Thy throne, O God, is for ever and ever: a sceptre of righteousness is the sceptre of thy kingdom.* This is a quote from Psalm 45:6, a Messianic Psalm, and He is called God. In John 1:1-4 we read, *In the beginning was the Word, and the Word was with God, and the Word was God. ²The same was in the beginning with God. ³All things were made by him; and without him was not any thing made that was made. ⁴In him was life; and the life was the light of men.* Then in verse 14 we see that He was God in the flesh; *And the Word was made flesh, and dwelt among us, (and we beheld his glory, the glory as of the only begotten of the Father,) full of grace and truth.*

He was the only begotten Son of God as John 3:16 states, "*For God so loved the world, that he gave his only begotten son, that whosoever believeth in him should not perish, but have everlasting life.*"

He came to save the world from their sins: John 1:29 "*The next day John seeth Jesus coming unto him, and saith, Behold the Lamb of God, which taketh away the sin of the world.*" Jesus Himself said in Luke 19:10 "*For the Son of man is come to seek and to save that which was lost.*"

So my question to you dear reader is, "Who do you say Jesus is?" Later in this chapter we will learn of the plan of salvation and you will see that Jesus is your only chance for heaven. Please understand, there is no way to heaven other than through Jesus Christ.

Ignorance of the Bodily Resurrection of Jesus Christ

It's necessary that I insert this topic in this book because there are pastors, (yes, I said pastors) who do not believe, nor will they teach the physical, bodily resurrection of our Lord and Savior, Jesus Christ. The latest poll I found was a Jeffrey Haddon poll which showed that 13% of Lutherans, 30% of Presbyterians, 33% of Baptists, 35% of Episcopalians and 51% of Methodist pastors did not believe in the physical, bodily resurrection of Jesus Christ. These are people who preach from pulpits every Sunday. How does one expect to have the anointing of God on himself if he is an unbelieving, hypocritical pastor who is, in essence, play acting the role of God's spokesperson? Well, you're wondering what the big deal is I suppose. The big deal is that if God didn't raise up Jesus Christ from the dead, then why would He raise up the believer from the dead? Is this an important issue? You bet it is! As I've stated before, the bible has to be believed. Not just by pastors, but by all who call themselves Christians. Unlike all other books, this one included, which can be argued as to its content, the bible is to be viewed as infallible, inerrant and inspired in order for it to be a help to an individual or a society. As far as the resurrection goes, the bible teaches very plainly that Jesus did, in fact, come out of that tomb and was seen by Mary Magdalene, the three women who went to anoint his body, then He appeared to His disciples. The apostle Paul told us in 1 Corinthians 15:5-8 "*5 And that he was seen of Cephas, then of the twelve: 6 After that, he was seen of above five hundred brethren at once; of whom the greater part remain unto this present, but some are fallen asleep. 7 After that, he was seen of James; then of all the apostles. 8 And last of all he was seen of me also, as of one born out of due time.*" Even the Jewish historian Josephus, stated in his text, "for he appeared to them alive again the third day; as the divine prophets had foretold these and ten thousand other wonderful things concerning him." Josephus was not born until 37 AD and did research to the fact that Jesus did rise from the dead and was indeed, seen by others. We cannot be too careful to not refute what God has said in His Word.

Ignorance of the Church

First of all, I want to set the record straight, that there is absolutely no church today that can lay claim to being the "first church." The New Testament settled that in Matthew chapter 16:16-18 when Peter acknowledged that Jesus Christ was the Son of the living God. Matthew 16:16-18 - *16 And Simon Peter answered and said, Thou art the Christ, the Son of the living God. 17 And Jesus answered and said unto him, Blessed art thou, Simon Barjona: for flesh and blood hath not revealed it unto thee, but my Father which is in heaven. 18 And I say also unto thee, That thou art Peter, and upon this rock I will build my church; and the gates of hell shall not prevail against it.*

There are those that will tell you that this is where Jesus ordained Peter as the first "Pope" or head of the church. However, a look at the Greek words used here will solve the problem once and for all. When Jesus said, *"thou art **Peter,**"* he used the Greek word *Petros,* meaning a stone, or a "piece of rock." But speaking of Himself, He then stated, *"and upon this rock I will build my church."* The word *"rock"* used here was *Petra,* meaning "a mass of rock, or a boulder." This in no wise implied that Peter was going to be the head of the church, although he was a leader in the church at Jerusalem.

The church was literally started at Pentecost when Peter preached in Acts chapter 2 and the Bible says that Acts 2:37 - *Now when they heard this, they were pricked in their heart, and said unto Peter and to the rest of the apostles, Men and brethren, what shall we do?* In verse 41 we read, *Then they that gladly received his word were baptized: and the same day there were added unto them about three thousand souls.* So, three thousand souls were added that first day to the church. Later on in verse 47 the bible says *"And the Lord added to the church daily such as should be saved."*

I have also had "discussions" with folks who state that the church didn't really start until Paul started preaching and Gentiles were getting saved. When I confronted him about this, he stated that the word *"**Church**"* in Acts 2:47 "didn't really mean 'church' as used elsewhere."

It's the same word used over and over again in the Bible for the church: *ekklēsia* meaning "a called out assembly." To state that any word in the bible doesn't really mean what it has said is to say one of two things. (1) Either 2 Timothy 3:16 is incorrect where it says, *All scripture is given by inspiration of God,* (emphasis mine) *and is profitable for doctrine, for reproof, for correction, for instruction in righteousness:* or (2) the Holy Spirit, through Luke when writing the Book of Acts "misspoke" when he called it a "church" in Acts 2:47. Of course it was the church plain and simple. Make no mistake about it.

I also would like you to notice that all who *"gladly received his word were baptized: and the same day there were added unto them about three thousand souls."* They were automatically put on the church rolls. There was no question about whether or not they should join the church. It was a "given" fact that they were *"added unto them."* The requirements for membership in the church were simple and twofold. Believe and be baptized. Following this, in verse 47 it says, *"and the Lord added to the church daily such as should be saved."* As William Evans states in his book, Great Doctrines of the Bible, "It's essential that the members of the early church be added 'unto the Lord' before they were added to the church."

Some churches will welcome people with open arms to their membership rolls without even finding out whether or not they have even been saved or baptized. This, in turn, gives the member a false sense of security and could cost him/her dearly in eternity.

Now I'm going to get to the "nitty-gritty" of the church and the common misconceptions surrounding it.

Why do people come to church? Why do you come to church? What is the church? What is the main function of the church?

First of all, let's define the word church. The church is not a building. When the Apostle John wrote the Book of Revelation, he wrote letters to the seven churches in Asia, or what was known as Asia Minor (which now comprises most of Turkey). But he was not writing to church buildings; He was writing to local assemblies of believers. In other words, he was writing to individuals who made up the local assemblies; in today's language, the pastor and members of the church.

The church was established, above all, for the honoring and exaltation of God. It is not now, nor ever was meant to be a social club. I have had people who were looking for a church call me and it seemed as if they were shopping for a church like they were shopping at Walmart or somewhere else. They didn't ask about our doctrine, our stance on spiritual or social issues and such. The questions were, "Do you have a fitness center?", or "What kind of after school programs do you have?" and other questions which had no bearing whatsoever on Jesus Christ. I'm not saying a church shouldn't have things like this, but first and foremost, a church should be a place where the Gospel is preached and Jesus Christ is exalted. It gets to the point nowadays that the average church is just like the church at Corinth. The church at Corinth was the most carnal, worldly church of that time. But the church at Corinth had nothing on the churches of today. The Christians at Corinth were doing nothing but looking out for themselves and that is exactly what the modern day Christian is doing. Christ was not being exalted in the church due to the selfishness of the rest of the members. Does this sound familiar in your church? If so, then something needs to be done to change it.

Every service conducted in the name of Christianity should be a Christ exalting, Christ honoring service. Too many times the services get twisted around and it seems that everything and everyone is being exalted except for the Lord Jesus Christ.

There are churches today that have more social activities than they do Bible based activities. These are the churches that will do anything as long as it draws a crowd. They have fishing trips, bowling tournaments, golf outings, blue jeans Sunday, etc, and people will turn out by the droves to attend these functions. But if you say you're going to have a Bible study, hardly anyone will show up. Once again, I lay the blame totally on the pastor. It is his responsibility to lead, and to lead in the proper direction. Once a pastor loses control of his authority, he may as well pack his bags, because he loses his respect along with the loss of authority.

Ignorance of the Plan of Salvation

If someone tells me they're saved, I always ask, "Saved from what?" Invariably their answer will be, "Oh yes, I'm going to heaven when I die!" I suppose in one sense of the word that is a correct response. But what you're really saved from is the penalty of your sins. It's hard to get a person to admit that he or she is a sinner bound for hell. They think that if they just say a prayer and ask God to save them, then everything will be fine. Not true!

In John chapter 3 and verse 3, it says, ***Jesus answered and said*** *unto him, Verily, verily, I say unto thee, Except a man be born again, he cannot see the kingdom of God.* Except a man be born again? What does that mean? He's talking about regeneration. It makes no difference as to whether you are a man, woman, boy or girl, president or pauper, nothing exempts you from the necessity of the New Birth. The bible is very clear that if you are not born again, you are lost. It's not something that we acquire on our own. It's a supernatural change imparted to us by God Himself when we ask Jesus Christ to save us. Understanding the New Birth will also assist you in understanding the change that salvation brings into one's life.

We are not saved to go on living the life we lived prior to receiving Jesus Christ as Lord and Savior. Paul tells us in 2 Corinthians 5:17 *Therefore if any man be in Christ, he is a new creature: old things are passed away; behold, all things are become new.* This is where the New Birth takes over in our lives. Jesus told Nicodemus in John 3:6, *"That which is born of the flesh is flesh…"* and it can never be anything else other than flesh. Then Jesus told Nicodemus *"and that which is born of the Spirit is spirit."* When we are reborn spiritually, we literally "die to sin" and undergo a "spiritual" rebirth. How is that done? The Word of God comes together with the Spirit of God to cause a conception. 1 Peter 1:23, says about the new birth *"Being born again, not of corruptible seed, but of incorruptible by the Word of God."* It's nothing we do on our own. It's solely an act of God in our lives. It's an inward, or heart change, that has outward results in our lives.

In order for one to be saved, you have to realize certain things. First of all, you have to understand that the only way to heaven is through Jesus Christ. He very plainly made this clear to us in John chapter 14 and verse 6, when He plainly stated to His disciples, *"I am the way, the truth, and the life: no man cometh unto the Father, but by me."* Secondly, you have to fully realize that you are a sinner. God's Word tells us in Romans 3:23 *For all have sinned, and come short of the glory of God.* You may say, "Well, I'm not as bad a person as "John Doe" over there. Maybe not. But if you and John Doe made a bet that you could jump across the Mississippi River who would win? You'd both get a running start, and jump with all your strength when you got to the river bank. You may have jumped a few feet farther than John Doe, but you both still missed the mark and wound up in the raging torrents of the river. Whether or not you believe that you are not as big a sinner as someone else has no bearing on getting you into heaven. We ought not to be comparing ourselves by human standards; we have to follow the standard set by God and not man. In Romans 5:12 the bible tells us, *Wherefore, as by one man* (Adam) *sin entered into the world, and death by sin; and so death passed upon all men, for that all have sinned*: We inherited our sin nature from Adam, and because we sinned, we are going to die someday. But God, in His infinite and divine mercy, has made an opportunity for us to enter His Kingdom. In Romans 5:8-9 we read, *⁸ But God commendeth his love toward us, in that, while we were yet sinners, Christ died for us. ⁹ Much more then, being now justified by his blood, we shall be saved from wrath through him.*

In order to be saved from the punishment of our sins, we must first realize that we are sinners, and that Christ died on the Cross of Calvary for our sins. John 3:16: *For God so loved the world, that he gave his only begotten Son, that whosoever believeth in him should not perish, but have everlasting life.* The key word there is "*believeth.*" Notice it doesn't say "whosoever worketh" or "whosoever doeth!" Nothing you can do will get you into heaven. You can't work your way there. Ephesians 2:8-9 is very clear about that. It says *⁸ For by grace are ye saved through faith; and that not of yourselves: it is the gift of God: ⁹ Not of works, lest any man should boast.* Salvation is free for the asking. Two reasons why we can't work our way to heaven. First, if we could work our way, then Jesus died on the Cross of Calvary for no reason at all. Secondly, once we got up to heaven, we would be asking each other, "Hey, what did you do to get up here? I did this or that!" We would be so caught up in our own deeds, that we'd completely forget all the love that Jesus had for us to die on the cross. Titus 3:5-7: *⁵ Not by works of righteousness which we have done, but according to his mercy he saved us, by the washing of regeneration, and renewing of the Holy Ghost; ⁶ Which he shed on us abundantly through*

Jesus Christ our Saviour; [7] That being justified by his grace, we should be made heirs according to the hope of eternal life.

So how do we receive this free gift? Romans 10:9-10 says, *[9] That if thou shalt confess with thy mouth the Lord Jesus, and shalt believe in thine heart that God hath raised him from the dead, thou shalt be saved. [10] For with the heart man believeth unto righteousness; and with the mouth confession is made unto salvation.*

As I mentioned before, it all boils down to one simple word; FAITH. *For by grace are ye saved through faith.* When the Philippian jailer asked Paul and Silas, *"Sirs, what must I do to be saved?* The simple answer he gave in Acts 16, *"Believe on the Lord Jesus Christ and thou shalt be saved..."* Just take God at his word, and claim His salvation by faith. Believe and you will be saved. If you've never been saved, why not do it now. Simply bow your head and ask God to save you in this manner: "Dear Lord, I know that I am a sinner, I believe Jesus died on the cross and shed His blood for my sins, was buried and rose from the grave. I ask you now Lord Jesus to come into my heart, and take away my sins, and save my soul. Change my heart and life Lord, to be what you want me to be! I thank you Lord for the forgiveness of my sins, your gift of salvation and everlasting life, because of Your mercy and grace! Amen.

Going along in this same vein, the question is often asked, "Can a saved person ever be lost again?" The answer without hesitation is emphatically "No!" When Jesus said *"That which is born of the flesh is flesh, and that which is born of the spirit is spirit,"* it means that we have the Holy Spirit which entered into us at our New Birth. In order to lose our salvation, the Holy Spirit in us would have to die. He (the Holy Spirit) being one-third of the God Head, or Trinity, would mean that God would have to die also. This is quite the impossibility because God is eternal. If we could lose our salvation, then Jesus Christ would again have to die on the cross for our sins once more. The bible says in 1 Peter 3:18 *"For Christ also hath once suffered for sins, the just for the unjust, that he might bring us to God, being put to death in the flesh, but quickened by the Spirit:"* Being "quickened by the Spirit" means that even though He died on the cross, He was made alive again by the power of the Spirit of God. My friends, if God quickens you, giving you the New Birth, nobody can take that away from you. Jesus said *"I give unto them eternal life"* and if it only lasts a day, or a week or even a year, then it's not eternal. It's only temporary. Jesus said in John 10:28-29 *"²⁸ And I give unto them eternal life; and they shall never perish, neither shall any man pluck them out of my hand. ²⁹ My Father, which gave them me, is greater than all; and no man is able to pluck them out of my Father's hand."* When we were dead in our trespasses and sins, there was no way that we could save ourselves. So using that logic, if we cannot save ourselves, what makes us think we can keep ourselves saved? The bible tells us in Ephesians 4 that once we are saved, we are *"sealed unto the day of redemption."* The Holy Spirit of God has sealed you in the mercy and grace of Almighty God and nothing or no one can break that seal. We were sealed at the time of our regeneration.

Let me also say something here about repentance. This is a matter that not too many pastors are preaching on these days either. Why? Because most people relate repentance to works, and as I said before, you cannot work your way to heaven. But just what is repentance. The Greek word for repent is μετανοέω or *metanoeō*. It's the word from which we get our word metamorphosis. Just like through metamorphosis a caterpillar changes into a butterfly, we turn from our wicked ways and start going in a Godly direction. It means "to think differently" or in plain language, to do an "about face" spiritually. Although works don't save you, only faith does, your faith should produce works. The Apostle James tells us in James 2:17-20 *"¹⁷ Even so faith, if it hath not works, is dead, being alone. ¹⁸ Yea, a man may say, Thou hast faith, and I have works: shew me thy faith without thy works, and I will shew thee my faith by my works. ¹⁹ Thou believest that there is one God; thou doest well: the devils also believe, and tremble. ²⁰ But wilt thou know, O vain man, that faith without works is dead?"* True salvation will produce a change of heart in any individual. You will definitely show evidence of your salvation by what you do from then on. Saving faith will turn people away from their sins and produce a desire to serve the Lord and produce fruit. If you have no desire to serve God, then I suggest you take a close look at yourself and your salvation to see if, indeed, you are truly saved. This is not to appear as being judgmental towards anyone. I definitely want people to be sure of whether or not they are truly saved. There's a saying that says the distance between heaven and hell is approximately 18 inches, which is the distance between your head and your heart. You may indeed, have a head knowledge of Jesus Christ, but is He truly in your heart. Be sure! Be very, very sure dear reader!

There will be a judgment coming for all of us one day. A glad day for some and a sad day for others. For some reason the idea that God would simply throw people into a flaming hell burning with fire and brimstone is unconscionable. I get asked all the time that "What kind of loving God would cast people into hell? What kind of God would do that?" The answer to that question is very simple. God does not "simply" cast people into hell. On the contrary, they do it to themselves. It's not God's will that any should perish. 2 Peter 3:9 *"**The Lord is not slack concerning his promise, as some men count slackness; but is longsuffering to us-ward, not willing that any should perish, but that all should come to repentance.**"* People reject the call of Christ in their lives and then they wonder why God judges them so harshly. Ladies and gentlemen, we have a God who is just. Because He is a just God, He cannot and will not allow sin to go unpunished. As I stated before, the bible tells us that we've *all sinned and come short of the glory of God.* People sit in churches all over the world, they hear about the love that God has for them and they still can't accept the fact that they're sinners and won't acknowledge the fact for one minute. In Romans 3:10, Paul tells us that *"**There is none righteous, no, not one.**"* The bible says that *the wages of sin is death* (Romans 6:23). Because we are sinners, we're going to die. If you've not experienced the New Birth, you're going to be judged. Hebrews 9:27 states, *"**And as it is appointed unto men once to die, but after this the judgment.**"* You are going to stand before God one day at the Great White Throne Judgment and you will then wish you had taken Jesus Christ more seriously in your life. Let me give you a brief preview of the facts concerning your judgment before God. The Book of Revelation gives a glorious depiction of heaven in chapter 21. But the very last verse of chapter 21 tells us who will and will not be there. It says in verse 27 *"And there shall in no wise enter into it any thing that defileth, neither whatsoever worketh abomination, or maketh a lie: but they which are written in the Lamb's book of life."* When you receive the New Birth, your name is written in the Lamb's Book of Life. It could be called the "heavenly roster" if you will. Things will get scary for those whose name is not written in the Lamb's Book of Life. In chapter 20, the bible describes this judgment to the fullest. Think dear reader, is this what you want to go through? Revelation 20:11-15 *"¹¹ And I saw a great white throne, and him that sat on it, from whose face the earth and the heaven fled away; and there was found no place for them. ¹² And I saw the dead, small and great, stand before God; and the books were opened: and another book was opened, which is the book of life: and the dead were judged out of those things which were written in the books, according to their works. ¹³ And the sea gave up the dead which were in it; and death and hell delivered up the dead which were in them: and they were judged every man according to their works. ¹⁴ And death and hell were cast into the lake of fire. This is the second death. ¹⁵ And whosoever was not found written in the book of life was cast into the lake of fire."* You may think that just because you have your name on a church roll somewhere, or just because you taught a Sunday school class at one time, or just because you were baptized, that you have a free ticket to heaven. The real question for you today is, "Do you have your name written in the Lamb's Book of Life?" The *"Second death"* talked about in verse 14 above is the spiritual death. An eternity without Jesus Christ. The bible says there will be weeping and gnashing of teeth. You had a physical birth from your birth mother, and you need a Spiritual birth from the Heavenly Father. Someone once so aptly stated, if you're born once, you die twice, but if you're born twice, you only die once. Why would you want to reject something like that when it is free for the asking? Heaven will be such a glorious place. It's yours for the asking. Here is a small sample of what you will experience in heaven. Revelation

21:2-5 *"² And I John saw the holy city, new Jerusalem, coming down from God out of heaven, prepared as a bride adorned for her husband. ³ And I heard a great voice out of heaven saying, Behold, the tabernacle of God is with men, and he will dwell with them, and they shall be his people, and God himself shall be with them, and be their God. ⁴ And God shall wipe away all tears from their eyes; and there shall be no more death, neither sorrow, nor crying, neither shall there be any more pain: for the former things are passed away. ⁵ And he that sat upon the throne said, Behold, I make all things new. And he said unto me, Write: for these words are true and faithful."* We have a God who loves us, cares for us and wants us to dwell in heaven with Him for all eternity. He wants to comfort us here in this life also. Peter, the great apostle said in 1 Peter 5:7 *"Casting all your care upon him; for he careth for you."* I cannot for the life of me understand why someone would reject an offer like that. You, the reader may say, "I don't believe it!" I choose to believe it. If I'm wrong, I've lost nothing. You choose not to believe. If you are wrong, you've lost everything. Some will take the brave attitude and say, "Well, I'm going to have a few things to say to God when I see Him." Not quite! The bible plainly states in Philippians 2:9-11 that *"⁹ Wherefore God also hath highly exalted him, and given him a name which is above every name: ¹⁰ That at the name of Jesus every knee should bow, of things in heaven, and things in earth, and things under the earth; ¹¹ And that every tongue should confess that Jesus Christ is Lord, to the glory of God the Father."* Sooner or later you, my friend will bow to Jesus Christ. You can do it now, or you will do it later. The choice is entirely yours. The bible has been far too accurate throughout the centuries not to be believed. The prophecies are there to see how they have been fulfilled.

Ignorance of the Ordinances of the Church

The first Ordinance of the church that I want to talk about is baptism. There are many misconceptions concerning this ordinance that we need to deal with scripturally. We will do it in love, but we will do it firmly with no apologies.

First of all, scripturally, baptism is a symbol of the death, the burial and the resurrection of Jesus Christ. The Catholic Church and the Lutheran Church call it a sacrament, meaning it saves you, or in their words "a means of receiving the grace of God.

In "The Catechism of the Catholic Church, Part 2, Article 1 (1213), it defines Baptism as follows: "Holy Baptism is the basis of the whole Christian life, the gateway to life in the Spirit *(vitae spiritualis ianua)*, and the door which gives access to the other sacraments. Through Baptism we are freed from sin and reborn as sons of God; we become members of Christ, are incorporated into the Church and made sharers in her mission: "Baptism is the sacrament of regeneration through water in the word."

The bible, however, teaches otherwise. The bible does not teach baptismal regeneration, nor does it even hint at baptismal regeneration. There is no saving power whatsoever in baptism. It is a symbol only. A symbol of the death, burial and resurrection of the Lord Jesus Christ. Romans chapter 6 and verse 4 plainly states *"Therefore we are buried with him by baptism into death: that like as Christ was raised up from the dead by the glory of the Father, even so we also should walk in newness of life."*

When I go out and witness to people and ask them if they are saved, invariably, some will run and get their baptism certificate and tell me that, "Yes, I've been baptized." They are holding on to a false sense of security by thinking that this certificate is their ticket to heaven. A study of the scriptures will show that baptism always comes after being saved. When Peter preached at Pentecost in Acts Chapter 2, we see in verse 41, *"Then they that gladly received his word were baptized: and the same day there were added unto them about three thousand souls."* When Phillip told the Ethiopian Eunuch about Jesus Christ we read in Acts 8:36-39 *"[36]And as they went on their way, they came unto a certain water: and the eunuch said, See, here is water; what doth hinder me to be baptized? [37]And Philip said, If thou believest with all thine heart, thou mayest* (emphasis mine). *And he answered and said, I believe that Jesus Christ is the Son of God. [38]And he commanded the chariot to stand still: and they went down both into* the water, both Philip and the eunuch; and he baptized him. *³⁹And when they were come up out of the water, the Spirit of the Lord caught away Philip, that the eunuch saw him no more: and he went on his way rejoicing."* Another example is when Peter went and preached to the Gentiles at Cornelius' house and they got saved in Acts 10:47, and he said, *"Can any man forbid water, that these should not be baptized, which have received the Holy Ghost as well as we?"* I could post many more scriptures, but they all prove the same thing, and that is that baptism comes only after one has been saved.

While speaking of the ordinances, we must also mention The Lord's Supper, or Communion as some may call it. But is it also a symbol? I believe that it is more than just a symbol of the broken body and shed blood of Jesus Christ. Once again, the Roman Catholic Church believes that when the priest offers the bread and wine, the bread actually becomes the body of Christ, and that the wine actually becomes the blood of Christ. However, partaking of the Lord's Supper or Communion, does not make one saved.

The Apostle Paul was very adamant about how we are to partake of this ordinance in 1 Corinthians 11. It seems as if we have become robots while partaking of the Lord's Supper. We sit there, waiting for the bread to be passed around, take it, wait for the pastor to tell you to go ahead and eat it. And then do the same with the cup. But Paul said in 1 Corinthians 11:29 *"For he that eateth and drinketh unworthily, eateth and drinketh damnation to himself, not discerning the Lord's body."* When you partake of the Lord's Supper, what are you thinking about? Golf? Fishing? Wishing church was over with so you can go home? Or are you truly thinking about what Jesus did for you on the cross of Calvary? Jesus Himself said in Luke 22:19 *"And he took bread, and gave thanks, and brake it, and gave unto them, saying, This is my body which is given for you: this do in remembrance of me."* When you take the bread, do you actually think about the broken body of Jesus? His body was broken for your sins. What do you think about when you take the cup? In the very next verse Jesus said *"Likewise also the cup after supper, saying, This cup is the new testament in my blood, which is shed for you."* When you partake of the cup, do you think about His shed blood, or do you wish that the cup was larger so you could have had a bigger drink? When Paul said, *"not discerning the Lord's body"* he means that we should have a total understanding of exactly what Jesus did for each and every one of us on the cross. But to add to that I believe we should also be aware that as Christians, we have the indwelling of the Holy Spirit and we should always be aware of that also. The Lord's Supper is a serious time of reflection for all Christians.

Ignorance of the Second Coming of Christ

Many Christians believe that the Rapture of the Church is an interchangeable expression for the Second Coming of Christ. Actually, the Second Coming of Christ comes after the Rapture of the Church. Paul tells us several times in the New Testament that Jesus Christ will soon be taking His church out of this world to live with Him forever. The most prominent verses are found in I Thessalonians 4, starting at verse 13, *"¹³ But I would not have you to be ignorant, brethren, concerning them which are asleep, that ye sorrow not, even as others which have no hope. ¹⁴ For if we believe that Jesus died and rose again, even so them also which sleep in Jesus will God bring with him. ¹⁵ For this we say unto you by the word of the Lord, that we which are alive and remain unto the coming of the Lord shall not prevent them which are asleep. ¹⁶ For the Lord himself shall descend from heaven with a shout, with the voice of the archangel, and with the trump of God: and the dead in Christ shall rise first: ¹⁷ Then we which are alive and remain shall be caught up together with them in the clouds, to meet the Lord in the air: and so shall we ever be with the Lord. ¹⁸ Wherefore comfort one another with these words.* It is plainly seen in this passage of scripture that we are being *"caught up together with them in the air."* It is going to be an instantaneous event that is so fast, it will be barely seen with the naked eye. The word *"caught"* in that verse is the Greek word ἁρπάζω *harpazo,* which means to "snatch up" or to pluck out. Something done in a very quick and speedy gesture. Paul also describes it in 1 Corinthians 15:52 where he states it will happen *"In a moment, in the twinkling of an eye, at the last trump: for the trumpet shall sound, and the dead shall be raised incorruptible, and we shall be changed."* Nowhere in these passages does it state that Jesus is coming down to set foot on the earth at that particular time.

The Book of Revelation is very specific as to when the Second Coming of Christ will be occurring. It says in Revelation chapter 19 that Jesus and His army will descend from heaven to do battle with the armies of the beast (Antichrist) and the false prophet. The bible says that a sword proceeded out of his mouth. This sword is nothing other than the Word of God. In verse 20, these two beings were cast into the *"lake of fire burning with brimstone."* Next we see in verse 21 that the remainder of the beast's army was slain by the sword proceeding out of His mouth. In other words, Jesus Christ spoke them into oblivion. In Revelation chapter 20 we see the devil and his angels cast into the bottomless pit for a thousand years. This is when Jesus Christ will begin His marvelous millennial reign with his saints from glory. Not until Jesus sets foot back upon the face of this earth does the "Second Coming of Christ" take place. Don't confuse the two events because they are very different.

Ignorance of the Purpose of Deacons

Why does a church have deacons? To speak for everyone else? To make decisions for the entire church? To keep the pastor in line? All of the above? I have been wondering about this for quite some time and I still have not found a valid reason for a church having deacons. Servants, yes; deacons, no! That is, deacons in the sense that they are utilized in today's churches. Yes, I know what you're thinking, but hear me out on this. "Deaconism" has gotten so out of hand in most churches today that absolutely no one has any say in the church except "the board." Some may think I am treading on the Holy Grail by my attitude towards deacons, but hear me out on this important matter. As one may probably see by now, I am writing this from a Baptist perspective, and we all know that Baptists feel that a church would collapse without the "divine" guidance of deacons. The principles, however, are all the same.

The problem with most churches, especially medium sized churches and above, is that, in general, most "deacon boards" are nothing more than a bunch of pompous incompetents who have no power anywhere other than the church. Nothing sends more chills down a pastor's spine sometimes than the words "Board of Deacons." But I want to take a Biblical look as to what a deacon is, and also, what he isn't.

At the very outset, I want to be perfectly clear in saying to all deacons who might be reading this, that "You do not run the church!" You may think that God has called you to be the standard bearer for all the church members and only you can decide what is best for all concerned. But that is not the case. For those of you who believe that the deacons run the church, please read on.

The main basis that churches use for the establishment of deacons is Acts chapter 6, verses 1-6. The problem with this is that nowhere in this passage of scripture is the word "Deacon," in the modern sense, mentioned. I would like for us to study this passage carefully in order to get a grasp on just what is going on here in Acts Chapter 6.

First of all, the church at Jerusalem was estimated to have somewhere between eighteen to twenty-five thousand members. There was a conflict going on between the Greek speaking Jews who did not speak Aramaic (the language of the Hebrews) and the Hebrews who spoke both Aramaic and Greek. The Grecian Jews felt that their widows were not being attended to properly by the church and brought the matter to the church leaders. Remember, this was the daily ministering of the church. The counseling, dealing with any problems which might (and always do) come up, and as we will see later, the preaching of God's Word. The apostles were busy studying the Word of God, going through the Old Testament Scriptures and praying. They didn't have the New Testament Scriptures as we do today. As a matter of fact, some of these men would go on to write nine of the New Testament Books.

So what did they do? They appointed seven men, who the Bible says were *"of honest report, full of the Holy Ghost and wisdom"* to do the daily administration of the church. In other words, the normal duties of what we would call a Pastor today. Why would someone need to be *"full of the Holy Ghost and wisdom"* if all they were going to do was "wait on tables"? The men they appointed were, as quoted in Acts 6:5, *"Stephen, a man full of faith and of the Holy Ghost, and Philip, and Prochorus, and Nicanor, and Timon, and Parmenas, and Nicolas a proselyte of Antioch."* All of these men were Greek, and we learn of only two of them; Stephen and Philip. When you read about Stephen, you will see that he was *"Full of faith and power, did great wonders and miracles among the people"* (Acts 6:8). Stephen was a preacher, make no mistake about it. He was eventually martyred for his service to the Lord Jesus Christ. When he had preached to the Jews, the bible says in Acts 7:54 that *"when they heard these things, they were cut to the heart, and gnashed on him with their teeth."* Then, later on down in Acts 7:57-58, *57 Then they cried out with a loud voice, and stopped their ears, and ran upon him with one accord, 58 And cast him out of the city, and stoned him: and the witnesses laid down their clothes at a young man's feet, whose name was Saul.* When we read of Philip, we see that he was not only a preacher, but a missionary and evangelist as well. In Acts 8:5 we see that he was a Missionary, for he *"went down to the city of Samaria, and preached Christ unto them."* We see him leading the Ethiopian Eunuch to a saving knowledge of Jesus Christ in Acts 8:37, and then in verse 38 he baptized him. Then we see that Philip was also an evangelist in Acts 21:8 where it says, *"And the next day we that were of Paul's company departed, and came unto Caesarea: and we entered into the house of Philip the evangelist, which was one of the seven; and abode with him."* This is hardly what I call *"waiting on tables."*

What about the other five men? Perhaps Prochorus was skilled in plumbing and maybe they made him a deacon and put him in charge of the maintenance around the church. Maybe Nicanor was a good cook, so they appointed him a deacon in charge of the fellowship suppers. How about Timon? Well, his family has been members of the church from the beginning, so it was only natural that he follow in his father's footsteps and become a deacon. He's not very regular in attendance either, but if we make him a deacon, maybe he'll come to church more often. Parmenas had a talent for music and they made him a deacon and put him in charge of the choir. Nicolas had a lot of money, so it made good sense to make him a deacon so he could make all the financial decisions for the church. Of course, all of this is said "tongue-in-cheek" but those seem to be the reasons why and how churches choose and appoint deacons today.

Stephen and Philip were preachers in every sense of the word and there is absolutely no reason to believe that the other five men weren't doing the exact same things. So my point here is, that if we are going to have "deacons" in the church, and we are going to use Acts 6 as the basis for our decision to have deacons, then whoever is appointed as a deacon needs to be a deacon in the true Biblical sense. Not for someone to just own a title, looking down his nose at the pastor or other church members, and do nothing for the cause of Christ.

One could also go to the other end of the spectrum on this. If, in fact, "deacons" were appointed in Acts 6, the only time you see the word is in verse 2 where it says, ***"Then the twelve called the multitude of the disciples unto them, and said, It is not reason that we should leave the word of God, and serve tables."*** The word *"serve"* in verse 2 is not an adjective, but a verb. It is the Greek word "διακονέω" (diakoneō). Its literal meaning is to "minister unto" or to "serve." It has no meaning of authority or power, nor does it grant such. So, you deacons can either be a preacher or a servant, but not sit in a seat of authority.

It's gotten to the point in some churches that deacons wield the "Hammer of Justice" and what they say is law. It's a spiritual nightmare for anyone to be the pastor of a "Deacon Possessed" church. More pastors have been run off, ousted and humiliated by deacon boards than any other problem in a church, simply because the deacons didn't know their proper place. I was actually told one time by a deacon, "The pastor is the spiritual leader, but the deacons run the church." Of course, when I asked for a Scripture to back that up, there was none to be found. Personally, I believe that churches today would be much better off without deacons and simply appoint committees to handle whatever problems come to the surface. I know of many churches that operate this way and it is a much smoother operation. You never see anywhere in the bible where it tells the local church to establish a board of deacons. As I stated earlier, the church at Jerusalem had somewhere between eighteen and twenty-five thousand members and yet they only appointed seven deacons (if, indeed, that is what they were). You will find some churches today who average less than one hundred people and they have more deacons than that. This is simply a tradition that we could well do without in our churches.

I will say that not all deacons are evil. On the contrary, I was in another church where I had absolutely no problems at all with the deacons and they literally bent over backwards to support me. Deacons who do know the true meaning of the title are a great blessing and a valuable asset to both the church and to the pastor.

Chapter 4

TOLERANCE

Tolerance is running rampant in churches today. When I say "churches" I am referring to all denominations and not just one or two denominations. Churches today seem to back away from things which might be considered "controversial" or not "politically correct" so as not to offend anyone.

Homosexuality

Once again, I have to express my godly love for these people but I also express my disdain for the lifestyle they are living.

The Episcopal Church took the lead in endorsing homosexuality by ordaining gay and lesbian priests. This has caused a great divide in the Episcopal Church all around the world. During the 2003 General Convention, the Episcopal Church, USA confirmed the consecration of Bishop Gene Robinson as bishop of New Hampshire. He was/is in a long term, committed relationship with another man.

Although not all in the leadership of the Episcopal Church endorses homosexuality, indeed, an overwhelming majority of them do not; they stated that they consider loving, committed same-sex relationships to be no different than similar heterosexual relationships.

Their so-called logic in this:

An article in the Houston Chronicle dated February 12, 2005, reported that between 100 and 200 couples would be united in marriage at the Resurrection Metropolitan Community Church in Houston, Texas. Several pastors from the local area participated in the ceremony. One of the pastors said "Go back 150 years and you'll find good Christians arguing on behalf of slavery, offering all sorts of biblical justifications. Go back a few years, and churches, including the Southern Baptists, argued against ordaining women," he said. "Not just time changes, but people change. I honestly believe God is doing something new here." Yes, the pastor was correct when he said that times change and people change. But he failed to mention another important fact stated in Malachi 3:6, "*For I am the Lord, I change not; therefore ye sons of Jacob are not consumed.*" Just because times change and people change, does not mean that God has changed. We need to be very careful if we attempt to speak for God, who has already spoken to us through His Word. He also stated that, "I honestly believe God is doing something new here." For him to make such an absurd statement that God would be doing this is an atrocity for which he will have to answer in judgment at the throne of God. God in no way shape or form would endorse something which He has already condemned.

Another pastor stated in the same article, "Some minds and hearts are not open to the great diversity of humankind — diversity created by God. God is all loving and merciful and cares a great deal for justice." Did you get that? This pastor stated that the "Diversity" i.e. homosexuality, was created by God. It seems as if this pastor has forgotten that God would never create something He calls an abomination. I question the fact that perhaps the pastor even knows that there is a force of evil in this world called Satan. But then again, they are playing right into Satan's hands. The pastor also stated that "God is all loving and merciful and cares a great deal for justice." Indeed, God does, in fact, care a great deal for justice. As a matter of fact, God is a "Just" God and because of His justice, Jesus Christ had to die on the cross to pay a huge penalty for our sin. Had he not done that, we would be facing God's justice at the Great White Throne Judgment.

I fear that pastors are not speaking out on this issue, especially now since we have a president who endorses same sex marriage and now the Supreme Court has thrown out The Defense of Marriage Act. Pastors, whether black or white, have a responsibility to stand up for Godly issues. If a pastor has a family in his church that has a loved one, friend or other relative involved in homosexuality, or has had an abortion, etc; that subject is NOT off limits on which to preach. Fear of offending, as mentioned before in chapter 1 is not an excuse for not preaching the whole Word of God!

With the issue of the transgender folks coming out of the woodwork and wanting to use the dressing rooms or restrooms of the gender that they "Identify" with is a troubling situation. It's already been proven that those who thrive on this perversion will use it to exploit their agenda. It's already happening where men, who "identified" as women have been caught in dressing rooms and restrooms taking photos with their cell phones unbeknownst to the ones being photographed. This is just the tip of the iceberg, and pastors need to remain staunch on this issue and keep their congregations informed about these important matters. A pastor friend of mine absolutely caught me off guard when he told me that he doesn't preach on homosexuality anymore because he has two families in his church that have children who are openly homosexual and are proud of that fact. Are we to not preach God's Word simply because people are living in open sin and it's not politically correct to speak out on it? You can preach the Word in a loving, thoughtful way, but to not preach the complete Word is a sin in itself. Paul talked about this in Philippians 3:19 when he stated *"**Whose end is destruction, whose God is their belly, and whose glory is in their shame, who mind earthly things).**"* These people are thinking only of themselves and their own lustful appetites. They are glorying in the things of which they should be ashamed.

Dr. Paul R. McHugh, the former psychiatrist-in-chief for Johns Hopkins Hospital and its current Distinguished Service Professor of

Psychiatry, said that transgenderism is a "mental disorder" that merits treatment, that sex change is "biologically impossible," and that people who promote sexual reassignment surgery are collaborating with and promoting a mental disorder. I continually pray that our country and our leaders will come to their senses and put an end to this as soon as possible.

The Southern Baptist Convention is also a very good example of tolerance. For years now, they have been standing around scratching their heads and wondering why their membership and offerings continue to go down. They have tried several different programs to boost membership and increase giving and all to no avail. They try to blame it on the economy, poor church attendance and a dozen other things, when the real problem is staring them directly in the face.

What I'm talking about here is Calvinism or "Reformed Theology." This is the idea that God has predestined some to be saved and some to be lost and condemned to hell, and there is nothing anyone can do about it. This is what is now known as "Reformed Theology." I like to call it "Deformed Theology." They adhere to the TULIP theology which is as follows:

TULIP Theology

TOTAL DEPRAVITY: Man is totally corrupt and dead and cannot respond to the gospel unless God sovereignly enables him. In other words, you are so sinful, that you don't realize that you're a sinner and God, if He wants you to be saved, will enlighten you to that fact. However, Romans 10:17 says, *"So then faith cometh by hearing, and hearing by the Word of God."* You can also see in John 1:12, *"But as many as RECEIVED him, to them gave he power to become the sons of God, even to them that believe on his name."*

UNCONDITIONAL ELECTION: God unconditionally chooses who will be called to salvation. Calvin believed that God also chooses who will go to hell. "[God] devotes to destruction whom he pleases and they are predestinated to eternal death without any demerit of their own, merely by his sovereign will. He orders all things by his counsel and decree in such a manner, that some men are born devoted from the womb to certain death, that his name be glorified in their destruction. ... God chooses whom he will as his children while he rejects and reprobates others" (Institutes of Christian Religion, Book III, chap. 23). Calvinism teaches that God selects who is going to be saved and who isn't. But the bible states that there is only one way to be saved. Ephesians 2:8: *"For by grace are ye saved through faith; and that not of yourselves: it is the gift of God."* In Luke 7, Jesus told the woman who anointed his feet with oil, *"Thy faith hath saved thee; go in peace."* In Acts 16:30-31 the Philippian jailer asked Paul and Silas, *[30] And brought them out, and said, Sirs, what must I do to be saved?* Notice what Paul and Silas told him in the very next verse, *[31] And they said, Believe on the Lord Jesus Christ, and thou shalt be saved, and thy house.*

LIMITED ATONEMENT: The death of Christ was only for those God will call to salvation. Calvin denounced the universal offer of the Gospel. "When it appears that when the doctrine of salvation is offered to all for their effectual benefit, it is a corrupt prostitution of that which is declared to be reserved particularly for the children of the church" (Institutes, Book III, chap. 22). What they are saying here is that Christ died only for the elect (the ones chosen by God to be saved). But the bible is very plain that Jesus died for all. 1 John 2:2: *"And he is the propitiation for our sins: and not for ours only, but also for the sins of the whole world."* In 2 Peter 3:9, it's very clear that God wants everybody to be saved. *The Lord is not slack concerning his promise, as some men count slackness; but is longsuffering to us-ward, not willing that any should perish, but that all should come to repentance.*

IRRESISTIBLE GRACE: God's call to the elect is effective and cannot be resisted. "That some, in time, have faith given them by God, and others have it not given, proceeds from his eternal decree; for 'known unto God are all his works from the beginning,' etc. (Acts 15:18; Ephesians 1:11). According to which decree he graciously softens the hearts of the elect, however hard, and he bends them to believe; but the non-elect he leaves, in his judgment, to their own perversity and hardness" (The Synod of Dort). Calvinism teaches that God's grace for salvation cannot be resisted. However the bible shoots several holes in that theory. When Stephen was preaching to the Jews at Jerusalem, he stung them with these words in Acts 7:51: *"Ye stiff-necked and uncircumcised in heart and ears, ye do always resist the Holy Ghost: as your fathers did, so do ye."* When Jesus was talking to the religious rulers in John 5:39-40, He told them, *"Search the scriptures; for in them ye think ye have eternal life: and they are they which testify of me. And ye will not come to me, that ye might have life."*

PERSEVERANCE OF THE SAINTS: Those who are elected and drawn will <u>continue</u> in the faith. The bible teaches "preservation" and not "perseverance." We read in 1 Thessalonians 5:23-24: *"And the very God of peace sanctify you wholly: and I pray God your whole spirit and soul, and body be preserved blameless unto the coming of our Lord Jesus Christ. Faithful is he that calleth you, who also will do it."* Also, over in John 10:27-29, Jesus seals the deal when He said, *"My sheep hear my voice, and I know them and they follow me: And I give unto them eternal life: and they shall never perish, neither shall any man pluck them out of my hand. My Father, which gave them me, is greater than all, and no man is able to pluck them out of my Fathers hand."*

I have studied the issue of Calvinism and cannot see any similarity at all with the Doctrine of Salvation by Grace through faith.

John Calvin, once a Roman Catholic until about 1530, was, with all due respect, a hateful and critical man when it came to those who disagreed with him. In a sermon on October 16, 1555, he referred to his enemies as "all that filth and villainy...mad dogs who vomit their filth against the majesty of God and want to pervert all religion. Must they be spared?"

I have heard the argument that, "Some of the greatest preachers in the world were Calvinists." That's also true. However, it's been a proven fact that not all Calvinists think alike. You have 5 point Calvinists, 4 point Calvinists and so on right down the line. Charles Spurgeon, one of the most prolific preachers of our time, was a Calvinist. He, however, caught the wrath of other 5 point Calvinists when he gave invitations and altar calls at his church. While Charles Spurgeon was an evangelistic Calvinist, for example, a large number of Calvinists of his day opposed him and denounced his broad, indiscriminate invitations for sinners to come to Christ. One Calvinist publication warned in Spurgeon's day, "... to preach that it is man's duty to believe savingly in Christ is ABSURD" (Earthen Vessel, 1857; cited in Spurgeon vs. the Hyper Calvinists by Iain Murray).

A pastor friend of mine addressed the issue of Calvinism at an Association meeting. He told the Director of Missions that he wanted it put in the record that his church is not, was not, and never will be a church that endorses Calvinism. The Director promptly told him that that was "too controversial a subject to deal with" and would not let him do it. I can't imagine a worse case scenario than the church not addressing something simply because it's controversial. Are we to be "Politically Correct" or "Biblically Correct"? Churches have split right down the middle on this issue and there seems to be no end in sight.

No other issue among Southern Baptist creates more furor in churches than this one. In my area alone, I know of 3 churches that have split right down the middle because of this issue. The largest Southern Baptist Seminary, Southern Seminary in Louisville, Kentucky probably turns out more Calvinist pastors than any other. In 2005, it was estimated that 60% of all graduates of Southern Seminary were Calvinists, and that number may very well be higher today.

The tragedy of this whole issue is that the leadership in the Southern Baptist Convention came out and formally addressed it at the Southern Baptist Convention held in Houston in June of 2013. In their *"Recommendations from the Committee on Calvinism,"* it was business as usual and virtually no action was taken, and doctrine took a back seat to tolerance and compromise. Thirteen times in the *"Recommendations"* it was stated that "We agree, but we differ." This issue is so divisive that someone at sometime is going to have to come out and say, "Enough is enough!" So far, I haven't seen anyone in the leadership of the Southern Baptist Convention who is willing to take that kind of a position on such a critical matter. What needs to happen is that someone needs to determine whether or not the Southern Baptist Convention is going to be a Calvinist entity or a Free Will entity. You can't have it both ways. Some would argue that, "We need the Calvinists." In reality, what they are saying is, "We need their money and support." Either you are going to be Calvinist organization or you're not going to be Calvinist organization. But at least have the courage to stand up and say one way or the other. If you put two stray tomcats in a box together, there's going to be a fight. That's exactly what's happening now with the Southern Baptists. The ones that are taking the lead and getting away from Calvinism are the smaller churches within the convention. They have cut down on their giving and some have even gotten completely out altogether. Sadly, the leadership of the Southern Baptist Convention is generally made up of large church pastors and leaders. They would do well to listen to some of the smaller churches. How in the world do they have the audacity to proclaim "The Great Commission Resurgence" which is to go out and evangelize, knowing full well that not one of the Calvinists believe it to be necessary?

Of course you will always have your "peacemakers" (bless them) who try and get folks to see things from both sides.

One Baptist Association that I know of in Alabama, at their Annual Meeting decided that they were going to accept the "traditional values" of the Southern Baptist Convention and not endorse Calvinism. All present voted to accept the resolution, but two churches "abstained" and didn't vote. Needless to say, these were the two largest churches in the Association. One of the churches that abstained has Sunday school classes for Calvinists and non-Calvinists. Go figure. Why would a church want to expound two totally different doctrines to their congregation?

There is just too much debate going on about this subject and it is taking a terrible toll on the cause of Christ. The best thing for all concerned is to part company. Let the Calvinists go their way and the rest of the Southern Baptist Convention go their way. There is altogether too much in-fighting among the leadership. In their arrogance, they have neglected to notice the failing programs, and the fact that the majority of the people don't want it. The ones who have spoken out on the issue like myself have been made to be the villains in this matter. I truly pray that they will see the need to go their separate ways and get down to the business of getting people saved.

While still speaking of the Southern Baptist Convention, let me state one more opinion which is an irritant to me and a number of other pastors. Anyone who has been a Southern Baptist for any length of time knows that "numbers" are a very important entity to them. They publish an annual publication which describes in detail how much each church gave the previous year, how many baptisms they had, how many are enrolled in Sunday School, etc. it seems that it is obsessed with these figures and it's a big talking point among the leadership. However, when talking finances and how much each church gives, this, like the tithe, should be an individual matter. They don't publish how much each individual church member gives, but they publish how much each church gives. You have large churches who give in the millions of dollars, and small churches who give in the hundreds of dollars, and then they rank them according to how much each one gave. It's really not any other churches business how much some other church gave. They are very open as to which church gave what, but very secretive in other areas of finance.

If you go to any Southern Baptist Church and look at their financial reports, each member is fully aware of how much each staff member is paid, because every member has a part in paying the pastor's salary, so it's common knowledge. The Southern Baptist Convention however, is very "hush hush" about their salary structure. Since every church has helped pay those salaries, they should be informed as to how much they are being paid. This goes along with what I stated in chapter one about how much money it costs to run the organization. I'm well aware that the President of the Southern Baptist Convention does not get a salary (but he gets an expense account), but all salaries should be open to the ones who pay them, i.e. the churches. I have been refused answers to these questions time and time again. It's time they came clean with the answers.

Tolerance of Sin in General

Many churches today have this mindset that once someone joins a church, whatever a person does after that is irrelevant, meaning that they don't want to bring shame to a church member or the church, so they tend to "overlook" some of the flaws and foibles of the individual. If someone is a deacon or a Sunday school teacher, or holds some other office within the church and they are living in sin or have done something to shame their testimony or the name of Christ, we overlook it so as not to start controversy within the membership. After all, that person is a Sunday school teacher and if we discipline him or her, they might get mad and leave, and then we have no one to fill that position. A pastor friend of mine told me he went to his "mentor" from college about a problem he was having in his church. The organist was having an affair with another member and he didn't know how to approach the church about it, so he asked one of his former teachers. The answer he got was, to say the least, shocking. The teacher asked him quite plainly, "Is this mountain worth dying on?" The fact that a former bible professor would say something like this used to be surprising. Not any more. Church discipline is rapidly becoming a thing of the past today. Too often pastors and churches turn a blind eye and a deaf ear to the ungodly goings on in their congregation for fear of losing some of the membership. It's included in this chapter on tolerance because that is exactly what it is; TOLERANCE. We have this idea that, sure, even though it was a sin years ago, maybe it's not so bad today. We have to be more open minded they say. My reply to that would be, "Would you stand in front of Almighty God and say that very same thing?" Probably not!

Relativism says that there are no absolute truths, in other words, "What may be alright to me may not be alright to you. All truth is subjective and may be subject to debate." Moral relativism says that what may be immoral for one is moral for another. The problem with this line of thinking is that it really doesn't matter what you think nor does it matter what I think. The only thing that matters is what God thinks. But then the relativism gurus will come back and say, "How do we know that the bible is true?" It's a vicious circle of a problem that only God can solve.

But getting back to the subject of church discipline, it is something that has been overlooked for some time now. The question for pastors and churches today is, "Are you going to be open-minded like the world, or are you going to do what God says to do and call it what it is? Sin! There are ways, biblical ways, to administer church discipline and they are constantly overlooked. Trust me on this because you will have people coming at you from both sides of the issue. People will tell you not to judge them, or we're living in the dark ages, or they'll just pack up and leave. On the other hand, you'll have other folks who like to fan the flames of discontent and say, "Are you going to allow that person to get away with this pastor?" Sometimes those people will also pack up and leave. I have always held to the idea that some people actually look better going then coming anyway. This should never be a cause for a pastor not to uphold biblical principles and standards in the church. When and if church discipline is necessary it should be done in a biblical manner. The first thing we need to remember is that membership in a local church, although necessary, is a privilege and not a right, and there are certain standards that God expects us to maintain as members of the body of Christ.

A pastor has an awesome responsibility to maintain discipline within the church body or chaos will surely ensue. Just as parents maintain discipline over their children, God expects the pastor to maintain discipline over His children, (i.e. the church). It's not a debatable point, it must be done. The church at Corinth had problems with fornication and they were trying to cover it up hoping it would go away, but it didn't. The Apostle Paul set them straight on the issue. They were trying to compromise to keep the peace, but it was an unsettling situation at best and a divisive one at its worst. Another thing to note here was that everyone in the church knew it went on and it was not information based on rumors or a "he said/she said" type situation. It was based on factual information. *Jesus gave us the basis for church discipline in Matthew 18:15-17* "**15 Moreover if thy brother shall trespass against thee, go and tell him his fault between**

thee and him alone: if he shall hear thee, thou hast gained thy brother.
16 But if he will not hear thee, then take with thee one or two more, that
in the mouth of two or three witnesses every word may be established.
17 And if he shall neglect to hear them, tell it unto the church: but if
he neglect to hear the church, let him be unto thee as an heathen man
and a publican." Unfortunately the church at Corinth didn't follow
these procedures and tried to sweep it all under the rug. Ladies and
gentlemen, you cannot compromise with sin. It is destructive to both
the individual and to the church. But let's not categorize every little
sin in the category of it needing church discipline. Please don't' run
to the pastor every time someone does something you don't think is
right. In most areas, we can agree to disagree. But when it is outright,
flagrant sin which has an adverse effect on the church's testimony, it
needs to be dealt with and dealt with swiftly. The best thing to do
is to get it out in the open, deal with it and go on with the business
of the church, which is expanding the Kingdom of Christ. If you
don't deal with it, take my word, it will sit there and fester like an
open sore. The longer you wait the worse it will get. Exercise church
discipline, but exercise it in the biblical way.

Chapter 5

HYPOCRISY

This final chapter is probably the most frustrating for me to put down on paper. As a pastor myself for the past 15 years, it greatly troubles me (or if I want to be 100% honest, it greatly angers me) to have to say some of the things I'm going to say here in this section.

When I speak of hypocrisy here in this chapter, I'm speaking of the everyday run of the mill Christian who commits sin. I'm also speaking of "pastors" who speak out of both sides of their mouths.

Concerning hypocrisy, we all know that every Christian everywhere lives in daily hypocrisy, because there's not a day that goes by when one doesn't commit some kind of sin; whether it's in thought or deed. When we do sin as Christians, however, we do have an advocate, who will provide forgiveness. The Apostle John, in preaching to Christians in 1 John 1:8-10 said, "*⁸If we say that we have no sin, we deceive ourselves, and the truth is not in us. ⁹If we confess our sins, he is faithful and just to forgive us our sins, and to cleanse us from all unrighteousness. ¹⁰If we say that we have not sinned, we make him a liar, and his word is not in us.*" So when people tell me they don't go to church because there are too many hypocrites there, I quickly tell them, "You're absolutely right, so come and join us. We can always use more." The key to a victorious Christian life is not so much not sinning, although we ought to try our best not to; the key to victory is the confessing of our sin.

Roman Catholics will go to a priest and confess their sin in the "confessional." This is not biblical and is contrary to God's Word. The Bible tells us in 1 Timothy 2:5, *"For there is one God, and one mediator between God and men, the man Christ Jesus."* We don't have to run to anyone here on earth because we have a direct line (so to speak) to God, through our Lord Jesus Christ. It's Him to whom we confess our sins. No human has the power nor the authority to forgive sin nor mete out punishment for sin.

In Old Testament times the Israelite went to the temple where there were many priests. The temple priests would offer up a sacrifice for the offender and that would be that. But Jesus Christ paid the ultimate price for our sins and the Bible tells us that He was the Sacrificial Lamb. In John 1:29, John the Baptist saw Jesus coming to be baptized and said, *"Behold the Lamb of God, which taketh away the sin of the world."* Only Jesus died for our sins, and only Jesus can forgive our sins.

In 1 John 1:9, the word *"confess"* is the Greek word ὁμολογέω, *homologeō*. It means to "agree with" God that it is sin. When confessing sin, call it what it is; sin! If you said a curse word, tell God you said a curse word. If you lusted in your heart, confess it and tell God you lusted in your heart. Don't just tell God, "Lord, I sinned. Please forgive me." When confessing our sin to God, we ought to confess it at the very moment we commit the sin. We ought not to wait and build up a "laundry list" and save them for when we have time to confess them. You didn't commit them all at once (hopefully) so you should not wait and confess them later all at one time. Unconfessed sin builds a wall of silence between you and God. There are no sins committed that God does not know about. You can't hide them from God. So you say, "Well, if He knows I did it, then why do I have to confess it?" Because God wants to hear it directly from you.

It's very hard in today's world for some reason, for a person to say, "I have sinned." In 2 Chronicles 7:14 the Bible says, *"If my people, which are called by my name, shall humble themselves, and pray, and seek my face, and turn from their wicked ways; then will I hear from heaven, and will forgive their sin, and will heal their land."* God's children, Israel, had sinned greatly before Him and were unrepentant. Look very carefully at the phrase, *"seek my face."* Why does God say that? Have you ever been wronged by someone and they came to apologize to you? Did they look you in the face when they apologized? Probably not! God wants you to look Him straight in the eyes and confess your sin by telling God exactly what it was that you did. That brings repentance. That brings humility and humility brings sacrifice. Hypocrites? Yes, definitely! Hopeless? Not a chance!

Hypocrisy in the Pulpit

Let me first start by saying that any pastor who does not believe 100% of God's Word, from Genesis 1:1 all the way through to Revelation 22:21, has no business whatsoever being in the pulpit preaching a watered down version of the Gospel of Jesus Christ. I'm stating this because there are, in fact, pastors out there who do not believe certain aspects of true Christianity. There are others who don't believe any of what they are "preaching." They are leeches feeding off the congregation thinking that they are doing them a huge favor by their presence in the pulpit. They also feed them false information about Christianity in their messages. Not outrightly, but just enough to cause a Christian to doubt their relationship with Jesus Christ. But they are very dangerous and sooner or later God will deal with these blasphemous creatures.

A study was published in 2010 by the Center for Cognitive Studies at Tufts University, under the direction of Daniel C. Dennett and Linda LaScola on *Preachers Who Are Not Believers*. They interviewed five unbelieving pastors and ministers who continue to serve their churches while hiding the fact that they no longer believed in God or the bible.

Dennett is a philosopher and cognitive scientist. According to the Oxford Dictionary, cognitive science is the study of thought, learning, and mental organization, which draws on aspects of psychology, linguistics, philosophy, and computer modeling.[4] He became a prominent figure in the atheist movement at the beginning of the 21st century. Linda LaScola is a clinical social worker, qualitative researcher and psychotherapist.

This was a study of five pastors from various denominations (Methodist, United Church of Christ, Presbyterian, Church of Christ, and Southern Baptist). In this study, two things were apparent about the five people involved. First, most attended liberal seminaries, and secondly, it was their professors in college who "instigated" their non-belief. A couple of them stayed in the ministry hoping that they would "sway" the thinking of their congregations. Others stayed in the ministry because they had nowhere else to go if they left. One of the persons interviewed even stated, "If someone would give me $200,000.00 right now, I'd turn in my resignation next week."

These types of preachers I'm afraid, are just the tip of the iceberg. There are pastors all over the country who believe nothing in the bible and are either just "making a living" for themselves, or trying to change the church into a non-believing entity. I say to all who are reading this book, Christians, beware! Peter warned us about these people in 2 Peter 2:1 *"But there were false prophets also among the people, even as there shall be false teachers among you, who privily shall bring in damnable heresies, even denying the Lord that bought them, and bring upon themselves swift destruction."* Peter said that there were false prophets in Israel's day but we don't have to worry too much about false prophets today so much. They are easy to pick out. The real problem is the false teachers. A false teacher is someone who knows the truth, but for some reason, mainly financial reasons, or wanting to please someone, he preaches something different. They normally preach what people want to hear as opposed to what they need to hear. These are very dangerous people and should be routed out of our churches as soon as possible. Don't be afraid to question your pastor on what you don't understand or about something he said. The best thing to do is to ask what he believes and go from there.

---

[4]   The Oxford Online English Dictionary 2016

It's important for church members to be fully aware of what their pastors do and do not believe. In my own denomination, pastors are selected by the church and not some hierarchy who appoints pastors like other denominations do. If you are in a church, it would be wise to ask your pastor what he or she believes. Ask them, "Do you believe that Jesus Christ was God in the flesh?" "Do you believe in the virgin birth of Jesus Christ?" "Do you believe that Jesus lived a sinless life while here on earth?" "Do you believe that Jesus died for everyone and not just 'the elect'?" "Do you believe in the physical bodily resurrection of Jesus Christ?" "Do you believe that the bible is the inspired Word of God?" "Do you believe in the inerrancy of the Scriptures?" These are just some of the questions you should be asking your pastor. If he or she stutters or stammers on any of the answers, you should dig deeper into their beliefs. If they answer "No" to any of the questions, my question to you would be, "Why are they still your pastor?"

There are other hypocritical people in pulpits all over this nation and the world making millions of dollars on television. The "Prosperity Gospel" preachers do more of a disservice to people than you can possibly imagine. These "Name It and Claim It" and "Blab It and Grab It" type pastors will tell you that if you send them money, God will bless you in a great way. Several have been identified as frauds. The only ones who are "blessed" as they put it, are the "pastors" themselves. They are making millions of dollars each year by preying on the unknowing who are desperate for some sort of miracle in their lives, and sometimes send their life savings in order to achieve that goal. Most of these televangelists have million dollar mansions, private jets and live in luxury at the expense of the poor people who sent them the money hoping for an answer to their prayers. One televangelist was exposed as a fraud when Primetime Live and Diane Sawyer found tens of thousands of prayer requests in a dumpster in one of his banks in Tulsa, Oklahoma. The televangelist never saw the prayer requests, but he certainly saw the money that accompanied them. Ladies and gentlemen it's not sinful to have money, but how you receive that money is another thing. Hear me on this; God doesn't "will" that everyone be rich and famous. As a matter of fact, God knows our hearts and knows that some of us, when becoming rich, will forget all about Him and His true will for each of our lives. If that were the case, why were none of the Apostles rich? They lived day to day trusting God to provide for their every need.

There are also "healing pastors" who prey on unknowing folks who are in search of a cure for their infirmities. They will pray over someone who is hoping for a cure and the only result is that the "evangelist" gets richer and the patient gets sicker. These are terrible tragedies which could be avoided through education. Don't misunderstand me, I believe in Divine Healing, but I don't believe in divine healers. If Benny Hinn, Peter Popoff and the likes of them were truly divine healers, why don't they go to every hospital in the world and heal everyone in them? The people brought up on those stages at the meetings are all screened before they come up. One was exposed as a fraud when, before a meeting, he had people fill out cards stating their infirmities. The cards were then given to a staff member who, in turn gave them to the televangelist's wife up in the sound room. The televangelist had a small receiver in his ear and his wife would transmit messages to him concerning certain individuals and their infirmities gleaned from all the cards taken up by staff members. He would act like he was receiving a "message from the Holy Spirit" and call out the infirmity and that person would come up on stage for "the cure." Is it God's will that everyone be in perfectly good health? No! If it was God's will for all to be healthy, why was Paul's "thorn in the flesh," which was probably his poor eyesight, not healed? He stated that he asked the Lord three times to heal him. Look what the Lord said in 2 Corinthians 12:8-10; *8 For this thing I besought the Lord thrice, that it might depart from me. 9 And he said unto me, My grace is sufficient for thee: for my strength is made perfect in weakness. Most gladly therefore will I rather glory in my infirmities, that the power of Christ may rest upon me. 10 Therefore I take pleasure in infirmities, in reproaches, in necessities, in persecutions, in distresses for Christ's sake: for when I am weak, then am I strong.* Sometimes God, in His infinite wisdom, puts us in situations to strengthen and renew our faith in Him. If we lived in a perfect world where there was no sickness, no heartaches and no sorrow, our human nature would kick in and if nothing went wrong, we would tend to forget that we have a God who loves us and cares for us. Take a look at yourself Christian. How many times do you think about God when things are going perfectly smooth for you in your life? Your job seemed perfect, and your family was healthy and you had plenty of money to fulfill all of your dreams. Was God on your mind much during those times? Now, think of how many times you doubted God when things weren't going so well. You lost your job, or you lost a loved one or your financial situation turned sour. I'm thinking you had God on your mind a lot more during those times than you did in the good times. The fact of the matter is we should have God constantly on our minds, whether in good times or bad times. That's why Jesus said He will call upon God and send us the "*Comforter*" in the person of the Holy Spirit.

Be very careful when you listen to these people. 1 John 4:1 tells us to "*try the spirits whether they are of God: because many false prophets are gone out into the world.*"

Trust me folks, there will be a tall pedestal for these people to stand on when they face the Great White Throne Judgment described in Revelation 20:11-14: *¹¹And I saw a great white throne, and him that sat on it, from whose face the earth and the heaven fled away; and there was found no place for them. ¹²And I saw the dead, small and great, stand before God; and the books were opened: and another book was opened, which is the book of life: and the dead were judged out of those things which were written in the books, according to their works. ¹³And the sea gave up the dead which were in it; and death and hell delivered up the dead which were in them: and they were judged every man according to their works. ¹⁴And death and hell were cast into the lake of fire. This is the second death.*

This book was a long time in the making because of a lot of prayer, soul searching, and research and, yes, illnesses and surgeries on my part. We as Christians need to take the lead to start making the main thing the main thing again in our churches and in our lives. This is something that didn't happen overnight and I realize that it isn't going to be fixed overnight. But something needs to be done, and done quickly. Jesus could come at any moment and millions of people will be left behind because of soft preaching, false preaching and "entertainment" in the name of Jesus Christ. It has to stop and we as Christians are the only ones who can.

We need to stop patronizing the churches who have the best entertainment but don't have any idea what the true gospel is. We need to get back to the basics of biblical preaching and preach God's Word as Paul instructed Timothy when he said in 2 Timothy 4:2-4 "*² Preach the word; be instant in season, out of season; reprove, rebuke, exhort with all longsuffering and doctrine. ³ For the time will come when they will not endure sound doctrine; but after their own lusts shall they heap to themselves teachers, having itching ears; ⁴ And they shall turn away their ears from the truth, and shall be turned unto fables.*" May I say that the time is already upon us when people will not endure sound doctrine, and have hired pastors who preach a real good, feel good message and have already turned away their ears from the truth and are turned unto fables? When I see these people being led like sheep to the slaughter it troubles me and breaks my heart. They are searching for the peace that only Jesus can give, and they think that just because a church has great entertainment, great enthusiasm, you feel good when you're told that everything is going to be ok, that this is the true church. Believe it or not it's not always the case that you should feel good when you hear a message from God. Some messages are meant to make you search yourself, some are meant to convict you of sin and some are indeed, meant to comfort. A large church doesn't necessarily mean that they are preaching the true Word of God, and a small church doesn't necessarily mean that they are not preaching the Word of God. Chances are the exact opposite is true. Sometimes there is a reason for the size difference, and that reason more often than not is that more people want to feel justified in their sins in showboat churches and not convicted of their sins in bible preaching, bible believing churches.

The choice is strictly up to you. This is definitely not to say that all large churches don't preach the true Word of God. One of my favorite, if not the favorite preacher of all time in my life was Adrian Rogers. He preached the Word unashamedly, unfalteringly and very profoundly. He also had a very large church in Belleview Baptist Church near Memphis, Tennessee. But God blessed his work there because he never put on a show. He never put himself in the limelight and it was ALWAYS Jesus Christ first and foremost in his services. He never tried to draw attention to himself like some other pastors do. If you are in a church where the pastor tries to put all the emphasis on himself, walk out the door and never look back. On the other hand, if the pastor is a Christ exalting pastor, honoring Jesus Christ, giving way to the leading of the Holy Spirit in every service, then consider yourself blessed to be there and pray for him at every opportunity, for that is the kind of church in which God expects His people to worship Him in spirit and in truth.

I hope that this book has enlightened you and caused you to think more about where you stand with the Lord Jesus Christ. If so, then it has done its job.

May God richly bless all of you who have read this book and I hope it blesses you, encourages you and helps you in your Christian walk.

Printed in the United States
By Bookmasters